HALIFAX
TRAVEL GUIDE

2024 Edition

Uncover the captivating history and cultural heritage of Halifax

Jim Baxter

TABLE OF CONTENT

Introduction

Welcome to the captivating city of Halifax, nestled along the picturesque shores of Nova Scotia's stunning coastline. As you embark on your journey through this comprehensive Halifax Travel Guide, prepare to immerse yourself in a world of rich history, breathtaking natural beauty, vibrant culture, and unforgettable experiences.

Halifax, the capital city of Nova Scotia, holds a unique place in Canada's maritime history. With a storied past that encompasses centuries of seafaring tales, Halifax has evolved into a modern and vibrant urban center that effortlessly blends its rich heritage with a contemporary spirit.

In this guide, we will take you on a captivating exploration of Halifax, offering you an insider's perspective on the city's must-see attractions, hidden gems, and local favorites. Whether you are a history enthusiast, an outdoor adventurer, a food lover, or a family seeking memorable experiences, Halifax has something for everyone.

Begin your journey by delving into Halifax's fascinating history. Explore iconic landmarks like Citadel Hill, a mighty fortress perched atop a hill, offering panoramic views of the city and a glimpse into its military past. Visit the Maritime Museum of the Atlantic, where you can discover the intriguing stories of Halifax's connection to the sea, including tales of shipwrecks and the city's role in the aftermath of the Titanic tragedy.

Beyond its historical treasures, Halifax boasts a thriving cultural scene. Delve into the world of art at the Art Gallery of Nova Scotia, showcasing maritime-inspired masterpieces.

Explore Pier 21, the Canadian Museum of Immigration, and gain insight into the personal stories of immigrants who arrived in Canada through Halifax. Immerse yourself in the vibrant performing arts scene at Neptune Theatre, where live performances captivate audiences year-round. And be sure to time your visit with the Halifax Jazz Festival, a celebration of music and culture that fills the city with rhythm and melodies.

The Halifax waterfront is a hub of activity, where you can witness the city's seafaring heritage come to life. Take a leisurely stroll along the Halifax Waterfront Boardwalk, lined with charming shops, lively pubs, and delightful seafood restaurants. Marvel at the majestic tall ships that dock along the harbor, providing a glimpse into Halifax's maritime traditions. And don't miss the opportunity to visit the Canadian Museum of Immigration at Pier 21, where the stories of countless immigrants who arrived in Canada are told with depth and emotion.

For those seeking outdoor adventures, Halifax does not disappoint. From the lush greenery of Point Pleasant Park to the rugged beauty of Peggy's Cove and the untouched wilderness of McNabs Island, nature lovers will find themselves spoiled for choice. Hike scenic trails, watch for whales in the open waters, or simply bask in the serenity of Halifax's natural landscapes.

No Halifax experience is complete without indulging in the city's culinary delights. Halifax's dining scene is a treat for the senses, with an abundance of fresh seafood, eclectic international cuisine, and local flavors. Whether you're savoring a lobster feast, exploring the North End's trendy eateries, sampling craft brews at a local brewery, or browsing the vibrant farmers' markets, Halifax promises to tantalize your taste buds and satisfy your cravings.

Throughout this guide, we will provide you with practical information, insider tips, and helpful resources to ensure your trip to Halifax is nothing short of extraordinary. Discover the best time to visit, find recommendations for accommodations that suit your preferences and budget, learn about transportation options, and familiarize yourself with essential phrases and local customs.

Halifax, with its captivating blend of history, culture, natural beauty, and warm maritime hospitality, invites you to embark on an unforgettable journey. Join us as we unveil the charms of this coastal gem and inspire you to create lasting memories in the vibrant city of Halifax.

Why You Should Visit Halifax

Rich History:

Halifax's history is palpable as you walk through its charming streets. The city's roots as a British settlement are evident in its well-preserved architecture and historic sites. Explore the iconic Citadel Hill, a star-shaped fortress that overlooks the city, and delve into the fascinating stories of Halifax's military past. Visit the Maritime Museum of the Atlantic, where you can discover the city's deep connection to the sea and learn about famous shipwrecks, the Titanic tragedy, and the city's role during times of war. Halifax's historic properties, including the Granville Mall and the Historic Properties Waterfront District, offer a glimpse into the city's vibrant past through their beautifully restored buildings and bustling shops.

Stunning Landscapes:

Halifax is blessed with breathtaking natural beauty that will leave you in awe. The city's picturesque waterfront is the perfect place to start your exploration. Stroll along the Halifax Waterfront Boardwalk, where you can enjoy stunning views of the harbor, admire tall ships, and indulge in delicious seafood from waterfront eateries. For nature lovers, Point Pleasant Park offers a peaceful escape with its winding trails, lush greenery, and panoramic views of the Atlantic Ocean. Don't miss the iconic Peggy's Cove, a charming fishing village located just a short drive from Halifax. Its rugged coastline, picturesque lighthouse, and unique rock formations make it a photographer's paradise.

Warm Maritime Hospitality:

Halifax is renowned for its friendly and welcoming atmosphere. The locals, known as Haligonians, take pride in their city and are always ready to share their love for Halifax with visitors. From striking up conversations at local pubs to offering recommendations on the best places to eat or visit, you'll quickly feel like a part of the community. Immerse yourself in the city's vibrant culture by attending festivals and events such as the Halifax Jazz Festival, the Buskers Festival, or the Nocturne Art at Night. These celebrations showcase the city's artistic spirit, local talents, and lively entertainment scene.

Activities for Every Visitor:

Whether you're a history enthusiast, an outdoor adventurer, a food lover, or a family seeking fun-filled activities, Halifax has something to captivate every visitor. History buffs can embark on guided tours that bring the city's past to life, or explore the numerous museums and historical sites at their own pace. Outdoor enthusiasts can hike scenic trails, kayak along the coast, or embark on thrilling whale-watching excursions. Food lovers will be delighted by Halifax's culinary scene, where you can savor fresh seafood, indulge in farm-to-table delights, and explore the vibrant craft brewery scene. Families will find a wide range of attractions, including interactive museums, parks, and outdoor adventures tailored to entertain and educate children of all ages.

Vibrant Arts and Culture Scene:

Halifax is a hub of creativity, arts, and culture. The city is home to a thriving arts community, with numerous galleries, theaters, and live music venues. Explore the Art Gallery of Nova Scotia, which houses an impressive collection of local and international artwork. Attend captivating theater performances at Neptune Theatre, showcasing a range of productions from classic plays to contemporary works. Halifax also hosts various cultural festivals throughout the year, such as the Halifax Pop Explosion and the Atlantic Fringe Festival, where you can immerse yourself in the city's vibrant arts scene.

Maritime Adventure and Water Activities:

With its coastal location, Halifax offers an abundance of maritime adventures and water activities. Embark on a scenic harbor cruise and enjoy panoramic views of the city's skyline from the water. For the more adventurous, try kayaking along the coastline, where you can explore hidden coves and encounter marine wildlife up close. Fishing enthusiasts can join a charter boat tour and try their hand at catching local species like mackerel or cod. The waters around Halifax also provide excellent conditions for sailing, allowing visitors to experience the thrill of navigating the Atlantic Ocean.

Day Trips to Charming Coastal Towns:

Halifax serves as a gateway to picturesque coastal towns that are well worth a visit. Take a short drive to Lunenburg, a UNESCO World Heritage Site known for its colorful wooden houses, charming waterfront, and rich seafaring history. Explore the Bluenose II, a replica of the famous schooner that graces the Canadian dime. Another delightful day trip option is Mahone Bay, famous for its iconic three churches and its quaint shops and art galleries. These nearby towns offer a glimpse into Nova Scotia's coastal charm and provide an opportunity to explore more of the province's maritime heritage.

In Halifax, the blend of captivating history, stunning landscapes, and warm maritime hospitality creates a unique and enchanting experience for every traveler. Whether you're seeking cultural immersion, outdoor exploration, culinary delights, or simply a relaxed coastal getaway, Halifax promises to exceed your expectations and leave you with cherished memories. So, get ready to embark on a journey of discovery and embrace the charms of this remarkable coastal gem.

A Brief Overview of Halifax's History:

Halifax boasts a captivating history that spans several centuries, shaped by the interactions between Indigenous communities, European settlers, and key historical events. Understanding Halifax's historical significance provides a deeper appreciation for the city's cultural fabric and the experiences it offers to visitors today.

Originally inhabited by the Mi'kmaq people for thousands of years, the Halifax region held great significance for their culture and way of life. The Mi'kmaq had a deep connection to the land and the surrounding waters, relying on them for sustenance and spiritual practices. Their presence in the area predates European settlement and contributed to the rich heritage of the region.

In the early 18th century, European settlement in the Halifax area began when the British established a fortified town in 1749. Named after the Earl of Halifax, who was then the President of the Board of Trade and Plantations, the town served as a strategic outpost for the British Empire in North America. Its location provided a sheltered harbor and access to the Atlantic Ocean, making it an ideal base for trade and naval operations

As Halifax developed, it quickly grew into a bustling hub for trade, attracting merchants, shipbuilders, and craftsmen from various parts of the world. The city became known for its shipbuilding industry, with countless vessels setting sail from its docks. The Royal Navy also established a strong presence in Halifax, using the city as a strategic naval stronghold during times of conflict.

However, Halifax has also witnessed its share of tragedies. One of the most significant events in the city's history occurred on December 6, 1917, when the Halifax Explosion shook the city to its core. A collision between two ships in the Halifax Harbour resulted in a massive explosion, causing widespread destruction and loss of life. It remains one of the largest non-nuclear explosions in history. The resilience and determination of the Halifax community in the aftermath of this devastating event became a defining characteristic of the city's spirit

Today, Halifax stands as a testament to its resilient past. Historic sites, museums, and landmarks throughout the city preserve the stories and heritage of the past, offering visitors an opportunity to delve into its rich history. The iconic Citadel Hill, a star-shaped fort overlooking the city, stands as a reminder of Halifax's strategic importance. The Maritime Museum of the Atlantic showcases the region's maritime heritage, including exhibits on the Titanic and the Halifax Explosion. Historic Properties, a collection of beautifully restored buildings, offers a glimpse into the city's architectural and cultural history.

From exploring the cobblestone streets of the Historic Properties district to learning about the city's role in World War II at the Halifax Citadel National Historic Site, visitors can immerse themselves in Halifax's fascinating history. The city's vibrant culture, friendly locals, and preservation of its past make it a destination that both educates and captivates travelers, allowing them to connect with the stories and experiences that have shaped Halifax into the coastal gem it is today.

Getting Around Halifax:

Navigating Halifax is a breeze, thanks to its efficient transportation system. Here are some key points to help you get around:

Halifax Stanfield International Airport:

Halifax Stanfield International Airport serves as the main gateway to the city of Halifax, connecting it to major cities across Canada and the United States. Located approximately 35 kilometers north of downtown Halifax, the airport offers a range of amenities and services to ensure a smooth travel experience for visitors.

Upon arrival at the airport, you'll find a variety of ground transportation options available to take you to your destination. Taxis are easily accessible outside the terminal, and friendly drivers can whisk you away to your hotel or any other location in Halifax. The taxi service operates on a metered fare system, and it is advisable to confirm the fare with the driver before starting your journey.

If you prefer shared transportation, shuttle services are also available at the airport. These shuttles offer convenient transfers to major hotels and popular destinations in the city. They provide a cost-effective option, especially for larger groups or those traveling with a significant amount of luggage.

For those who prefer the freedom of having their own vehicle, several car rental companies have counters at the airport. Renting a car allows you to explore Halifax and its surrounding areas at your own pace. The rental process is straightforward, and you can choose from a wide selection of vehicles to suit your needs. Whether you're planning to explore the city, venture into the countryside, or embark on a scenic road trip along Nova Scotia's coastline, having a rental car gives you the flexibility to create your own itinerary.

Public Transportation:

Halifax boasts a reliable and efficient public transportation system operated by Halifax Transit. Buses and ferries provide convenient access to different neighborhoods, attractions, and suburban areas, making it easy to navigate the city without a car.

The bus network covers a vast area, serving various routes throughout Halifax and its surrounding communities. Buses are equipped with comfortable seating, and many have features like Wi-Fi and USB charging ports. The fare system operates on a pay-per-ride basis, and you can purchase tickets directly from the bus driver or opt for a reloadable transit pass, which offers convenience and cost savings for frequent travelers.

One of the highlights of Halifax's public transportation system is the MetroX bus service. These express buses connect Halifax with nearby communities, offering a seamless commuting experience for residents and a convenient way for visitors to explore beyond the city limits. The MetroX service is particularly useful for day trips to charming towns and scenic areas outside of Halifax, such as Peggy's Cove or the Annapolis Valley.

In addition to buses, Halifax also has a ferry service that operates across the harbor. The Halifax-Dartmouth Ferry is a popular mode of transportation, providing a scenic and enjoyable journey between the downtown areas of Halifax and Dartmouth. The ferry offers a unique perspective of the city's skyline and waterfront, making it a favorite among both locals and tourists.

Downtown Halifax

Downtown Halifax is a compact and pedestrian-friendly area that invites exploration on foot. Its grid-like layout, well-marked streets, and numerous attractions make it easy to navigate and discover the city's vibrant atmosphere.

As you stroll through the historic streets of downtown Halifax, you'll encounter a delightful mix of charming architecture, unique shops, inviting cafes, and a wide range of dining options. The city's rich history comes alive as you pass by historic landmarks, such as St. Paul's Anglican Church, the oldest Protestant church in Canada, or Province House, the birthplace of parliamentary democracy in Canada.

The Halifax Waterfront Boardwalk is a must-visit destination in downtown. Stretching for 4 kilometers along the harbor, it offers breathtaking views, lively street performers, and an array of shops and restaurants. Take a leisurely walk along the boardwalk, and immerse yourself in the maritime ambiance while enjoying the fresh sea breeze. You can also hop on a harbor cruise or join a sailing tour to explore the waterfront from a different perspective.

Downtown Halifax is also a hub for cultural attractions and entertainment. The Art Gallery of Nova Scotia showcases an impressive collection of local and international art, while the Discovery Centre offers interactive exhibits and educational experiences for all ages. The vibrant entertainment district features theaters, live music venues, and pubs, providing a lively nightlife scene.

Taxis and Rideshares:

If you prefer the convenience of door-to-door transportation, taxis are readily available throughout Halifax. Taxi stands can be found at popular tourist spots, hotels, and transportation hubs, or you can hail a cab on the street. Taxis in Halifax are metered, and the fares are regulated, ensuring transparency and fair pricing. It's always advisable to confirm the estimated fare with the driver before starting your journey.

For a more contemporary transportation option, rideshare services such as Uber and Lyft operate in Halifax. These app-based services allow you to request a ride with just a few taps on your smartphone. Rideshares are particularly convenient for travelers who prefer the ease of cashless transactions and the ability to track their driver's arrival.

Car Rentals:

For travelers who desire the freedom and flexibility to explore Halifax and its surrounding areas at their own pace, car rentals are readily available in the city. Halifax Stanfield International Airport and downtown locations house several car rental companies, offering a wide selection of vehicles to suit different preferences and budgets.

Renting a car allows you to easily access the city's attractions and also venture into the picturesque countryside of Nova Scotia. From the iconic Peggy's Cove to the charming coastal towns of Lunenburg and Mahone Bay, having a rental car gives you the freedom to create your own itinerary and explore the stunning landscapes at your leisure. Just make sure to familiarize yourself with the local traffic rules and regulations, and consider obtaining a GPS or using a navigation app to help you navigate the roads.

Cycling:

Halifax is a bike-friendly city, with dedicated cycling lanes and trails that provide an enjoyable and environmentally-friendly way to explore the city's scenic routes. Renting a bike is a popular option for both locals and visitors who wish to experience Halifax's natural beauty and vibrant neighborhoods from a different perspective.

Several bike rental shops can be found throughout the city, offering a range of bicycles suitable for different ages and skill levels. Whether you choose to ride along the Halifax Waterfront Trail, which stretches for kilometers along the coast, or explore the Chain of Lakes Trail, which winds through scenic parks and lakeside communities, cycling in Halifax allows you to immerse yourself in the city's stunning landscapes and enjoy the invigorating outdoors.

It's worth noting that Halifax has implemented bike-sharing programs, where you can conveniently rent a bike for short periods and return it to designated docking stations. This option is perfect for quick trips or spontaneous rides around the city.

With a well-connected airport, reliable public transportation, a walkable downtown area, convenient taxi and rideshare services, car rental options, and a bike-friendly infrastructure, getting around Halifax is a breeze. Choose the mode of transportation that best suits your preferences and embark on a memorable journey through this captivating coastal gem. Whether you're exploring the city's historic sites, venturing into the picturesque countryside, or simply enjoying the vibrant atmosphere of downtown Halifax, the city's transportation options ensure that you can navigate with ease and make the most of your Halifax travel experience.

Here are a few popular apps that provide information about the transportation system in Halifax:

Transit App: Transit App is a comprehensive public transportation app that covers multiple cities, including Halifax. It provides real-time information on bus and ferry schedules, as well as estimated arrival times. The app also offers trip planning features, service alerts, and live updates to help you navigate the Halifax Transit system efficiently.

Google Maps: Google Maps is a widely used navigation app that offers detailed information about public transportation options in Halifax. It provides step-by-step directions for bus routes, including estimated travel times and schedules. The app also displays real-time updates on bus arrivals and departures, making it easy to plan your journeys in Halifax.

Moovit: Moovit is another popular transit app that offers comprehensive information about public transportation networks in Halifax. It provides real-time bus and ferry schedules, route planning, and live updates on service disruptions. Moovit also offers multimodal trip planning, allowing you to combine different modes of transportation, such as buses, ferries, and walking, to reach your destination.

Halifax Transit App: The official Halifax Transit App, developed by the Halifax Regional Municipality, provides real-time bus and ferry information, schedules, and route planning features. It offers a user-friendly interface and allows you to save your favorite routes and stops for quick access. The app also provides service alerts and updates from Halifax Transit.

Uber and Lyft: Both Uber and Lyft operate in Halifax, offering convenient ride-hailing services. By downloading the respective apps, you can request a ride, track your driver's arrival, and make cashless payments. Uber and Lyft also provide fare estimates, ensuring transparency and convenience for your transportation needs in Halifax.

These apps are available for download on iOS and Android devices. They offer valuable information and features to help you navigate Halifax's transportation system, whether you're using public transportation, taxis, rideshares, or planning your own routes with a rental car or bicycle.

As you embark on your Halifax adventure, keep in mind that the city's charm lies in its diverse neighborhoods and surrounding areas. Exploring beyond the city center allows you to discover hidden gems, picturesque coastal landscapes, and charming communities that add depth to your travel experience.

Historic Halifax: Tracing the City's Past

Citadel Hill: Halifax's Iconic Landmark

Perched majestically above the charming city of Halifax, Citadel Hill stands as an iconic symbol of the region's storied history and military heritage. This historic landmark is home to the Halifax Citadel National Historic Site, a remarkable star-shaped fortification that dates back to the 18th century. As visitors ascend the hill, they are treated to awe-inspiring panoramic views of the city's skyline and the picturesque harbor below, a sight that has captivated both locals and travelers for centuries.

Stepping onto Citadel Hill is like stepping back in time. The fort's ramparts, cannons, and defensive ditches transport visitors to an era when Halifax played a crucial role in the defense of British North America. Immerse yourself in the fascinating world of military history as costumed interpreters bring the stories and traditions of the Citadel to life. These knowledgeable guides offer captivating tales of the fort's strategic significance, the soldiers who served there, and the challenges they faced.

One of the highlights of any visit to the Citadel is the daily firing of the Noon Gun. This longstanding tradition, which dates back to the 1800s, reverberates throughout the city, marking the precise moment when midday arrives. As the resounding boom echoes across Halifax, it serves as a reminder of the Citadel's enduring presence and the rich heritage it represents.

Inside the Citadel, visitors have the opportunity to explore its well-preserved interiors, which provide a glimpse into the daily lives of the soldiers who once occupied the fort. Traverse the winding passageways and uncover the stories held within its walls. The Citadel's museum houses a wealth of artifacts, uniforms, and interactive exhibits that delve deeper into Halifax's military past. Discover the weapons and tools used by soldiers throughout the ages, learn about the intricacies of military strategy, and gain insight into the lives and experiences of those who served on Citadel Hill.

As you wander through the exhibits, you'll gain an appreciation for the sacrifices made by the men and women who defended Halifax. From the early days of the fort's construction to its role in significant historical events, such as the American Revolutionary War and the War of 1812, the Citadel holds a wealth of stories waiting to be uncovered. The museum's displays provide a tangible connection to the past, allowing visitors to reflect on the hardships and triumphs of the soldiers who once stood on this hallowed ground.

Beyond its historical significance, Citadel Hill offers a breathtaking backdrop for exploration and contemplation. The fort's elevated position provides commanding views of Halifax, with its vibrant cityscape and bustling harbor stretching out before you. Take a moment to soak in the beauty of the surroundings, capturing the perfect photograph or simply pausing to appreciate the majesty of the landscape.

For those seeking a deeper understanding of the Citadel's history, guided tours are available to provide in-depth narratives and insights into the fort's construction, strategic importance, and the battles it witnessed. Expert guides will regale you with tales of the various conflicts and sieges that shaped the region's past, bringing to life the struggles and triumphs of the soldiers who called the Citadel home.

Visiting Citadel Hill is an experience that transcends time, allowing visitors to connect with Halifax's rich heritage in a tangible way. Whether you're a history enthusiast, a military buff, or simply someone who appreciates panoramic views and captivating stories, the Halifax Citadel National Historic Site offers an unforgettable journey into the past. As you explore its ramparts, encounter costumed interpreters, and delve into the museum's exhibits, you'll gain a deeper appreciation for the indelible mark that the Citadel and its soldiers have left on Halifax's history.

Maritime Museum of the Atlantic: Unveiling Maritime Heritage

Situated along the vibrant waterfront, the Maritime Museum of the Atlantic stands as a captivating testament to Halifax's deep-rooted maritime heritage. As you step inside, you embark on a fascinating journey through the annals of history, delving into stories of shipwrecks, naval battles, and the courageous individuals who dared to venture into the unpredictable waters of the Atlantic.

The museum's collection is a treasure trove of artifacts that provides an intimate glimpse into the maritime past of Halifax. One of the most notable exhibits is dedicated to the tragic tale of the RMS Titanic. Discover personal belongings and items recovered from the wreckage, evoking a poignant sense of the human stories and the immense tragedy that unfolded on that fateful night in 1912. From a worn leather suitcase to a delicate pocket watch frozen in time, these artifacts serve as tangible connections to the lives lost and the enduring fascination with the ill-fated luxury liner.

In addition to the haunting tale of the Titanic, the Maritime Museum of the Atlantic chronicles the devastating Halifax Explosion of 1917, one of the largest non-nuclear explosions in history. Through immersive exhibits and historical accounts, visitors gain insight into the catastrophic event that forever changed the landscape and lives of Halifax residents. Explore the profound impact of the explosion, which resulted from a collision between two ships in the busy harbor, and learn about the heroic efforts of first responders and the remarkable resilience of the community in the face of unimaginable tragedy.

As you navigate the museum's corridors, you encounter a remarkable collection of model ships, each meticulously crafted and brimming with historical significance. These miniature vessels offer a glimpse into the grandeur and diversity of maritime craftsmanship, showcasing the evolution of shipbuilding over the centuries. Marvel at the intricate details of the models, ranging from majestic tall ships to sleek steamships, and appreciate the artistry and craftsmanship that went into their creation.

The Maritime Museum of the Atlantic also invites visitors to explore the fascinating world of navigational instruments. From early compasses to astrolabes and chronometers, these tools were instrumental in guiding sailors across the treacherous seas. Learn about the methods employed by navigators to chart their course, and gain an appreciation for the precision and expertise required to navigate vast oceans with only the stars and the tools at their disposal.

A visit to the museum wouldn't be complete without an exploration of Halifax's longstanding connection to the sea through its exhibits on fisheries and seafaring traditions. Gain an understanding of the vital role fishing played in the region's economy and cultural identity. Discover the techniques employed by fishermen, the challenges they faced, and the resilience that defined their way of life. Interactive displays and informative exhibits transport visitors back in time, offering a glimpse into the world of fishing communities and the significance of the maritime industry to Halifax's development.

Throughout the Maritime Museum of the Atlantic, the spirit of Halifax's seafaring legacy is palpable. It serves as a poignant reminder of the city's reliance on the sea and the enduring relationship between the people and the waters that surround them. The museum's commitment to preserving and sharing this maritime heritage ensures that the stories of Halifax's brave sailors, fishermen, and shipbuilders continue to resonate with visitors from around the world.

As you wander through the exhibits, you can't help but feel a profound sense of admiration for the individuals who embarked on perilous journeys, faced formidable challenges, and shaped the maritime history of Halifax. The Maritime Museum of the Atlantic pays homage to their courage, sacrifices, and resilience, reminding us of the profound impact the sea has had on the city's identity. It is a place where the past comes alive, where stories of triumph and tragedy intertwine, and where visitors can immerse themselves in the captivating narratives of Halifax's maritime heritage.

Halifax Public Gardens: A Victorian Oasis

Halifax Public Gardens is a haven of tranquility nestled in the heart of the bustling city, offering visitors a delightful escape into a world of natural beauty and Victorian charm. Since its establishment in 1867, these enchanting gardens have captivated the hearts of locals and visitors alike, providing a serene retreat from the fast pace of urban life.

As you step through the gates of Halifax Public Gardens, you are greeted by a symphony of colors and scents that permeate the air. Winding pathways beckon you to explore the meticulously manicured lawns, vibrant flowerbeds, and captivating displays of horticulture. This Victorian-style garden reflects the elegance and grandeur of a bygone era, creating a timeless oasis of peace and serenity.

Stroll along the winding pathways that meander through the gardens, taking in the ever-changing tapestry of blooms. From the delicate petals of roses and tulips to the vibrant hues of azaleas and dahlias, the gardens offer a kaleidoscope of colors that shift with the seasons. Each meticulously curated flowerbed and well-manicured shrubbery is a testament to the skill and dedication of the gardeners who tend to this horticultural masterpiece.

At the heart of the gardens stands the stunning Victorian-inspired bandstand, an architectural gem that serves as a centerpiece for both visual and auditory delights. During the summer months, the bandstand comes alive with the harmonious melodies of live music performances. Visitors can find respite on one of the nearby benches, allowing the soothing melodies to wash over them while basking in the tranquil ambiance.

One of the most enchanting features of Halifax Public Gardens is the serene ornamental pond, graced by graceful swans that glide effortlessly across its glassy surface. The gentle ripples of the water create a mesmerizing display, reflecting the vibrant blooms and lush greenery that surround it. Find a quiet spot near the pond, and let the soothing sounds of nature wash away the worries of the outside world.

Beyond the visual splendor and calming atmosphere, Halifax Public Gardens offers ample opportunities for relaxation and recreation. Find a cozy spot on the soft grass, spread out a picnic blanket, and indulge in a leisurely feast amidst nature's embrace. Take a moment to peruse a book, engage in conversation, or simply bask in the sunlight as the gentle breeze rustles through the leaves overhead.

The gardens also provide an ideal setting for a romantic rendezvous. The idyllic ambiance, punctuated by the fragrance of flowers and the delicate melodies of songbirds, sets the stage for intimate moments and cherished memories. Whether it's a leisurely hand-in-hand stroll, a serene boat ride on the pond, or a cozy picnic for two, Halifax Public Gardens offers a picturesque backdrop for love to blossom.

Halifax Public Gardens isn't just a place of quiet contemplation; it's also a hub of community engagement and celebration. Throughout the year, the gardens come alive with a variety of cultural events and activities that bring people together. From art exhibitions and photography contests to horticultural workshops and gardening seminars, there's always something to engage the senses and foster a sense of community among visitors.

For those seeking respite from the everyday hustle and bustle, the Halifax Public Gardens provide an oasis of serenity and natural splendor. Whether you're an avid horticulture enthusiast, a nature lover, or simply in search of a peaceful haven, these gardens offer an opportunity to disconnect from the demands of daily life and reconnect with the beauty of the natural world.

So, take a leisurely stroll along the winding pathways, marvel at the vibrant floral displays, and find solace in the harmonious symphony of nature. Halifax Public Gardens invites you to escape the bustling city and immerse yourself in a realm of tranquility and breathtaking beauty, where time seems to stand still, and worries melt away amidst the vibrant tapestry of colors and the gentle whispers of the wind.

Historic Properties: Preserving Halifax's Architectural Gems

In the heart of downtown Halifax lies Historic Properties, a charming waterfront district that invites visitors to step back in time and immerse themselves in the city's architectural heritage. As you wander through its cobblestone streets, lined with beautifully restored buildings, you'll find yourself captivated by the rich history and stories that each structure has to offer.

The buildings of Historic Properties stand as living testaments to Halifax's past, preserving the architectural styles that were prevalent during different eras. From Georgian to Victorian, the facades showcase the craftsmanship and attention to detail that characterized their construction. As you stroll along the streets, take a moment to appreciate the intricate details of the facades, the elegant windows, and the carefully restored elements that transport you to a bygone era.

One of the highlights of Historic Properties is the Granville Mall, a vibrant pedestrian zone that breathes new life into the historic district. This bustling promenade offers a delightful shopping experience with its unique shops, galleries, and boutiques housed within the historic structures. Here, you can browse through an eclectic array of artisanal crafts, local artwork, clothing boutiques, and specialty stores. Whether you're searching for a one-of-a-kind souvenir or a piece of handmade jewelry, the Granville Mall offers a treasure trove of options.

As you explore the Granville Mall, you'll notice a vibrant energy that fills the air. Street performers captivate passersby with their talents, creating a lively atmosphere that adds to the charm of the district. Take a moment to pause and enjoy their performances, whether it's a lively musical performance or a captivating street magician. The Granville Mall becomes a hub of activity, where locals and visitors come together to celebrate art, culture, and community.

Historic Properties is not just a place for shopping and browsing; it's also a culinary destination that showcases Halifax's renowned seafood offerings. Along the waterfront, you'll find a delightful selection of restaurants that tempt your taste buds with fresh Atlantic seafood delicacies. Indulge in succulent lobster, plump scallops, or perfectly cooked fish, all while enjoying the scenic views of the harbor. The combination of delectable cuisine, waterfront ambiance, and historic surroundings creates a truly unforgettable dining experience.

Throughout the year, Historic Properties transforms into a vibrant venue for cultural events and festivals. From lively music performances to art exhibitions, the district comes alive with creativity and celebration. The cobblestone streets and historic buildings serve as the backdrop for these events, adding an extra layer of charm and authenticity. Whether you're attending a music festival, an outdoor art show, or a cultural celebration, you'll be immersed in the lively atmosphere that seamlessly merges Halifax's past and present.

Historic Properties also offers a glimpse into the city's maritime heritage through its connection to the waterfront. As you explore the district, you'll come across historic wharves and docks that once bustled with activity. These waterfront areas were vital to the city's economy, serving as ports for ships that traded goods and connected Halifax to the world. Today, these waterfront areas have been repurposed into inviting spaces where visitors can enjoy the views, watch sailboats glide across the water, or simply soak in the peaceful ambiance of the harbor.

In addition to its architectural and cultural offerings, Historic Properties provides a gateway to other attractions in downtown Halifax. Located within walking distance are renowned landmarks such as the Halifax Waterfront Boardwalk, the Canadian Museum of Immigration at Pier 21, and the bustling Spring Garden Road. This central location makes Historic Properties an ideal starting point for exploring the city, as you can easily venture out and discover more of Halifax's treasures.

As the sun sets over the waterfront and the lights illuminate the buildings of Historic Properties, the district takes on a magical ambiance. The historic facades are bathed in a warm glow, creating a picturesque scene that is perfect for an evening stroll. The combination of the architectural beauty, vibrant atmosphere, and captivating history makes Historic Properties a true gem in the heart of Halifax.

Whether you're a history enthusiast, a lover of architecture, a shopping connoisseur, or a seafood aficionado, Historic

Properties offers something for everyone. Step into this enchanting district, and allow yourself to be transported to a different era, where the past seamlessly merges with the present, and the stories of Halifax's heritage come to life.

Halifax Citadel National Historic Site: Safeguarding the City's Defenses

The Halifax Citadel National Historic Site stands tall and proud, overlooking the vibrant city of Halifax and serving as a testament to the city's military significance. Built between 1828 and 1856, the Citadel was designed to protect the harbor and the city from potential invasions, reflecting the strategic importance of Halifax as a key naval outpost in North America.

As you approach the imposing stone walls of the Citadel, you'll immediately sense the aura of history that surrounds this impressive fortification. Step through the gates and into a world frozen in time, where the past comes alive through interactive exhibits, informative displays, and engaging demonstrations.

Wander through the labyrinthine tunnels that crisscross beneath the fort, once bustling with soldiers and supplies. These subterranean passageways were essential for the Citadel's defense, allowing for swift movement and strategic positioning. As you explore these tunnels, you can almost hear the echoes of the past and imagine the bustling activity that took place within.

Make your way to the barracks, where soldiers once lived, trained, and prepared for battle. Step inside the recreated living quarters and gain insight into the daily routines and challenges faced by the men who called the Citadel their home. Through carefully curated exhibits, you'll learn about the soldiers' uniforms, weaponry, and the hardships they endured while stationed at the fort.

To truly immerse yourself in the experience, be sure to participate in the interactive demonstrations that offer a glimpse into the lives of the soldiers. Marvel at the precision and skill of the 78th Highlanders, who perform stirring bagpipe and drum ceremonies, transporting you to a time when these musical traditions resonated through the fort. Witness the drill demonstrations, where soldiers showcase their military training and discipline, providing a captivating window into the life of a soldier in the 19th century.

Climb to the ramparts, where commanding views of the city, harbor, and surrounding landscape await. From this vantage point, take in the breathtaking panoramic vistas that stretch as far as the eye can see. Imagine the watchful eyes of the soldiers who stood guard atop these ramparts, vigilant in their duty to protect Halifax from any potential threats.

Inside the fort, immerse yourself in the immersive exhibits that showcase the Citadel's rich history. Discover artifacts, photographs, and stories that bring the past to life, highlighting the fort's strategic role in protecting Halifax and the soldiers who defended it. Learn about the challenges they faced, the battles they fought, and the innovations in military technology that shaped their tactics.

As you delve deeper into the Citadel's history, you'll gain a profound appreciation for the engineering marvels of its time. The Citadel's design incorporated advanced defensive features, such as a dry moat, drawbridge, and intricate masonry, reflecting the ingenuity and craftsmanship of the 19th-century military architects and engineers.

Beyond the historical significance, the Halifax Citadel National Historic Site is also a vibrant community space that hosts a variety of events throughout the year. From summer concerts and military reenactments to evening ghost tours and festive celebrations, there's always something happening within the Citadel's walls, ensuring that visitors of all ages can engage with history in unique and captivating ways.

A visit to the Halifax Citadel National Historic Site is a journey back in time, where the sights, sounds, and stories of the past come alive. It's an opportunity to explore a fortification that played a crucial role in Halifax's history and to gain a deeper understanding of the soldiers who defended the city. Whether you're wandering through the labyrinthine tunnels, witnessing the precision of the 78th Highlanders, or taking in the panoramic views from the ramparts, the Citadel offers an immersive experience that transports visitors to a bygone era.

Halifax Central Library: A Modern Architectural Marvel

While Halifax boasts a rich history, it also embraces contemporary architectural marvels, such as the Halifax Central Library. This award-winning structure blends seamlessly into the cityscape while redefining the concept of a public library. Step inside this vibrant hub of knowledge and creativity, where modern design principles converge with innovative technology.

Halifax Central Library stands as a testament to the city's commitment to fostering intellectual growth, community engagement, and the pursuit of knowledge. Located in the heart of downtown Halifax, this architectural masterpiece captures the imagination from the moment you lay eyes on its striking facade. Designed by world-renowned architecture firm Schmidt Hammer Lassen, in collaboration with local firm Fowler Bauld & Mitchell, the library's aesthetic brilliance harmonizes with its functional purpose.

Admire the striking architecture that features cascading wooden staircases, expansive windows that flood the space with natural light, and inviting communal areas for reading and socializing. The library's exterior is a captivating blend of glass and steel, with its unique shape and angles captivating the attention of passersby. The use of sustainable materials and energy-efficient design principles also highlights the library's commitment to environmental stewardship.

As you enter the library, you are welcomed by an open, airy atrium that serves as the heart of the building. The grandeur of the space is accentuated by the three-story-high wooden staircase, an architectural marvel that not only connects the different levels but also serves as a gathering spot for visitors. The library's interior design seamlessly combines functionality with aesthetic appeal, creating an atmosphere that invites exploration and discovery.

Browse an extensive collection of books, periodicals, and multimedia resources, catering to a wide range of interests and age groups. From classic literature to contemporary bestsellers, from academic journals to children's picture books, the library's collection reflects the diverse needs and tastes of its patrons. Well-organized shelves and comfortable seating areas make it easy to lose oneself in the world of literature, while cozy reading nooks tucked away in corners offer intimate spaces for quiet contemplation.

But the Halifax Central Library is not merely a traditional repository of books; it is a space where the analog and digital worlds converge. Step into the cutting-edge IdeaLab, a dedicated space for technological exploration and innovation. Here, you can immerse yourself in the digital realm, accessing a multitude of online resources, e-books, and digital archives. State-of-the-art computer workstations, interactive displays, and high-speed internet connectivity enable visitors to engage with technology and unleash their creativity.

Beyond its impressive collection and technological offerings, the Halifax Central Library serves as a dynamic community space. Its multifunctional rooms and auditoriums provide venues for workshops, lectures, and public events. From author readings and book signings to art exhibitions and film screenings, the library is a cultural epicenter that brings people together and fosters intellectual and artistic dialogue.

Visitors can participate in a variety of educational and enrichment programs designed for all ages. Engage in writing workshops, learn a new skill through hands-on craft sessions, or attend informative lectures on a range of subjects. The library also hosts book clubs, language exchange groups, and children's storytime sessions, nurturing a love for learning and creating a sense of community.

Halifax Central Library's commitment to inclusivity and accessibility is evident throughout the building. It features ramps, elevators, and designated spaces for individuals with mobility challenges, ensuring that everyone can fully access the library's resources and services. Additionally, the library offers programs and resources for individuals with visual or hearing impairments, promoting equal access to knowledge and cultural experiences.

The library's dedication to sustainable practices extends beyond its architectural design. It incorporates energy-efficient systems, such as geothermal heating and cooling, and employs sustainable materials and construction methods. The rooftop garden not only provides a serene outdoor space but also helps with rainwater management and supports biodiversity in an urban environment.

Halifax Central Library stands as a testament to the city's commitment to education, culture, and community. It is a place where the old and the new, the traditional and the innovative, seamlessly coexist. Whether you are seeking a quiet corner to read, access to digital resources, or engaging in lively discussions and workshops, the library offers an inclusive and inspiring environment for all.

As you immerse yourself in the vibrant atmosphere of the Halifax Central Library, you'll discover that it is not just a building but a living, breathing entity—a testament to the power of knowledge, creativity, and community.

As you delve into these historic sites, you'll gain a deeper appreciation for Halifax's cultural legacy and the significant role it has played in shaping the region's history. From the towering Citadel Hill to the immersive exhibits of the Maritime Museum, the Victorian oasis of Halifax Public Gardens to the architectural gems of Historic Properties, each landmark offers a unique window into the city's past and a chance to walk in the footsteps of those who came before.

Cultural Delights: Museums, Galleries, and Festivals

Halifax is a city that thrives on its vibrant cultural scene, offering a range of museums, galleries, and festivals that captivate visitors and locals alike. Immerse yourself in the artistic and creative spirit of Halifax with these cultural delights.

Art Gallery of Nova Scotia: Showcasing Maritime Art

Located in the heart of Halifax, the Art Gallery of Nova Scotia stands as a testament to the city's vibrant art scene and cultural heritage. As you step into the gallery's welcoming space, you are immediately enveloped in a world of artistic masterpieces that beautifully capture the essence of maritime life.

The Art Gallery of Nova Scotia boasts an extensive collection that showcases a diverse range of works from both local and international artists. However, what sets this gallery apart is its special emphasis on maritime-inspired art. With Halifax's deep-rooted connection to the sea and its rich maritime history, it is only fitting that the gallery pays homage to this integral aspect of the region's identity.

As you wander through the gallery's halls, you'll encounter a captivating array of artworks that evoke the mesmerizing allure of the ocean and the rugged beauty of the coastline. The stunning seascapes, rendered with meticulous attention to detail, transport you to the shores of Nova Scotia. Each brushstroke captures the play of light on the water, the graceful movement of sailboats, and the tumultuous power of crashing waves.

Beyond the maritime-themed pieces, the Art Gallery of Nova Scotia also embraces a broad spectrum of artistic styles and genres. From classic oil paintings to innovative mixed media installations, the collection encompasses a rich tapestry of creative expression. The gallery strives to create a space that both honors traditional forms of art and pushes the boundaries of contemporary artistic practices.

One of the highlights of the gallery is its collection of Indigenous artwork. The Art Gallery of Nova Scotia actively seeks to represent and celebrate the artistic traditions and perspectives of Indigenous communities in the region. Through these works, visitors gain insight into the deep cultural connections between the Indigenous peoples and the land and sea that have shaped Nova Scotia's history.

In addition to its permanent collection, the Art Gallery of Nova Scotia hosts rotating exhibitions that bring fresh and exciting perspectives to the forefront. These exhibitions often feature the works of emerging artists, providing them with a platform to showcase their talents and contribute to the ever-evolving artistic landscape of Halifax.

To enhance the visitor experience, the gallery offers educational programs, guided tours, and interactive workshops. These initiatives aim to foster a deeper understanding and appreciation of the artworks on display. Whether you are a seasoned art enthusiast or a curious beginner, the Art Gallery of Nova Scotia provides a welcoming and inclusive environment that encourages exploration, dialogue, and personal connections with the art.

Beyond the walls of the gallery, the influence of the Art Gallery of Nova Scotia extends into the community through outreach programs and collaborations. The gallery actively engages with local schools, community groups, and artists, aiming to inspire creativity and nurture a love for the arts among individuals of all ages and backgrounds.

For those seeking a memorable cultural experience in Halifax, a visit to the Art Gallery of Nova Scotia is an absolute must. It is a place where beauty and inspiration converge, where the region's rich artistic heritage is preserved and celebrated. Whether you find yourself captivated by the timeless allure of maritime-themed artworks or intrigued by contemporary pieces that challenge conventions, the gallery offers a captivating journey through the artistic soul of Nova Scotia.

As you exit the Art Gallery of Nova Scotia, you carry with you the echoes of brushstrokes, the vivid colors, and the profound emotions evoked by the artworks. You leave with a deeper appreciation for the artistic endeavors that reflect the spirit of Halifax and the enduring connection between the land, the sea, and the people who call this place home. The Art Gallery of Nova Scotia invites you to be inspired, to explore, and to be moved by the power of art.

Pier 21: Canada's Immigration Museum

Step into the history of Canadian immigration at Pier 21, often referred to as the "Ellis Island of Canada." Located in Halifax, Nova Scotia, this fascinating museum holds a special place in the hearts of millions of Canadians whose ancestors embarked on a transformative journey through its doors. Pier 21 tells the captivating stories of the immigrants who arrived in Canada through the port of Halifax, seeking new opportunities and a fresh start in a land filled with promise.

As you enter Pier 21, you embark on a poignant and immersive experience that brings the immigration process to life. The museum's interactive exhibits, personal testimonies, and carefully curated artifacts offer a profound glimpse into the diverse cultural fabric of Canada, shaped by the dreams, struggles, and triumphs of countless individuals.

One of the most striking aspects of Pier 21 is its dedication to preserving personal stories. Through oral history interviews and archival materials, the museum captures the voices of immigrants, providing an intimate understanding of their experiences. These firsthand accounts offer a deeply human perspective, transcending statistics and documents to reveal the emotional journey of leaving one's homeland and embarking on a new life.

The exhibits at Pier 21 guide visitors through the various stages of the immigration process. From the moment of arrival, visitors can explore the journey of newcomers as they disembarked at Halifax's iconic port. The museum showcases artifacts such as trunks, suitcases, and personal belongings that evoke the hopes and aspirations of those who sought a better future on Canadian soil.

One of the most moving aspects of Pier 21 is the re-creation of the Immigration Hall, where immigrants were processed and screened upon arrival. Walking through this meticulously reconstructed space, visitors can imagine the mix of emotions that filled the air as families were reunited, anxieties were felt, and dreams were realized.

Interactive exhibits allow visitors to engage with the stories on a deeper level. From virtual reality experiences that simulate the voyage across the Atlantic to interactive stations where visitors can explore the diverse cultures that have shaped Canada, Pier 21 encourages a sense of connection and empathy.

The museum also sheds light on the challenges and hardships faced by newcomers. Exhibits explore the cultural, linguistic, and economic barriers that immigrants encountered, emphasizing the resilience and determination that propelled them forward. Through photographs, letters, and personal mementos, visitors gain a profound understanding of the sacrifices made and the obstacles overcome in pursuit of a better life.

Pier 21 goes beyond the stories of individual immigrants; it celebrates the broader contributions made by immigrant communities to Canadian society. Exhibits highlight the vibrant traditions, arts, cuisine, and customs brought by diverse groups who have enriched the cultural tapestry of Canada. Visitors can explore the ways in which these communities have shaped the nation's identity, fostering an appreciation for the multiculturalism that defines Canada today.

The museum also recognizes the important role of immigration in shaping Canada's economic and social development. It showcases the contributions made by immigrants in various fields, from entrepreneurship to the arts, sciences, and sports. By illustrating the indelible impact of immigrants, Pier 21 promotes a deeper understanding of the integral role they have played in building the country.

Pier 21 is not just a museum; it is a place of reflection, remembrance, and celebration. It is a testament to the resilience, courage, and spirit of those who left their homelands to start anew. The museum offers a space for visitors to contemplate their own family histories, to connect with the stories of others, and to appreciate the shared experiences that bind us all.

Throughout the year, Pier 21 hosts special events, workshops, and educational programs that engage visitors of all ages. From lectures by guest speakers to cultural celebrations, the museum fosters dialogue, understanding, and a sense of community.

Pier 21 stands as a monument to the millions of immigrants who passed through its gates, a place where their journeys are honored and their stories are told. It serves as a reminder of the importance of compassion, empathy, and inclusivity in a world shaped by migration.

For anyone seeking to understand the profound impact of immigration on Canada's past, present, and future, a visit to Pier 21 is an essential experience. Step into this remarkable museum and let the personal narratives, interactive exhibits, and artifacts transport you through time, offering a profound and moving glimpse into the diverse cultural fabric of Canada.

Neptune Theatre: Live Performances in the Heart of the City

For theater enthusiasts, a visit to Neptune Theatre is an absolute must when exploring the vibrant cultural scene of Halifax. Situated in the heart of downtown Halifax, Neptune Theatre has been delighting audiences since its establishment in 1963. With its diverse repertoire of plays and musicals, this esteemed theater provides a captivating and immersive experience for all theater lovers.

Neptune Theatre has gained a reputation for its commitment to artistic excellence and its ability to showcase a wide range of theatrical genres. Whether you have a penchant for classic dramas, contemporary comedies, or Broadway-style productions, Neptune Theatre has something to offer that will undoubtedly captivate and engage you.

One of the remarkable aspects of Neptune Theatre is its commitment to supporting and showcasing local talent. The theater actively collaborates with both emerging and established artists from Halifax and the broader Atlantic Canadian region, giving them a platform to showcase their skills and creativity. This dedication to nurturing local talent fosters a vibrant and dynamic arts community, ensuring that Halifax's unique artistic voice is represented on stage.

As you step into Neptune Theatre, you'll immediately notice its intimate and inviting ambiance. The theater's seating arrangement ensures that every seat in the house offers an optimal view of the stage, allowing you to feel fully immersed in the performances. The carefully designed space creates an intimate connection between the audience and the actors, heightening the emotional impact of the performances and making for a truly immersive theater experience.

The repertoire at Neptune Theatre is diverse and carefully curated, catering to a wide range of tastes and interests. Whether you're drawn to the timeless classics of Shakespeare, the thought-provoking contemporary works, or the rousing energy of musicals, Neptune Theatre strives to present a balanced and varied program that appeals to theater enthusiasts of all backgrounds.

Throughout the year, Neptune Theatre hosts a variety of productions that span the theatrical spectrum. You might find yourself transported to the dramatic world of a

Shakespearean tragedy, where passion and betrayal unfold on the stage. Alternatively, you might be treated to an uproarious comedy that has the audience in stitches. And then there are the captivating musicals that bring captivating stories to life through song and dance, leaving you humming the tunes long after the final curtain call.

In addition to its main stage productions, Neptune Theatre also hosts special events, workshops, and readings that provide opportunities for both artists and theater enthusiasts to engage more deeply with the craft. These events offer glimpses into the creative process, allowing audiences to gain a deeper understanding of the art of theater and the dedication that goes into bringing stories to life on stage.

Furthermore, Neptune Theatre has also been recognized for its commitment to accessibility and inclusivity. The theater offers audio description and sign language interpretation services for select performances, ensuring that individuals with visual or hearing impairments can fully engage with the productions. This dedication to inclusivity is a testament to Neptune Theatre's belief that the transformative power of theater should be accessible to all.

Beyond its contributions to Halifax's cultural landscape, Neptune Theatre holds a special place in the hearts of the local community. For many residents, attending a production at Neptune Theatre is a cherished tradition, a night out that promises both entertainment and a sense of community. It serves as a gathering place where people come together to share in the magic of live theater and connect with one another through shared experiences and emotions.

When planning your visit to Halifax, be sure to check Neptune Theatre's schedule and reserve your tickets in advance. Whether you're a seasoned theater enthusiast or simply curious about exploring the performing arts, Neptune Theatre promises an unforgettable experience that showcases the immense talent and creativity that Halifax has to offer. Prepare to be swept away by the power of storytelling and the thrill of live performances in this vibrant and intimate theater nestled in the heart of downtown Halifax.

Halifax Jazz Festival: A Celebration of Music and Culture

Get ready to groove to the rhythm of Halifax's vibrant music scene at the Halifax Jazz Festival. Held annually during the summer, this renowned event brings together jazz enthusiasts and music lovers from around the world for a celebration of music, culture, and creativity. With its eclectic lineup of renowned jazz artists, local talents, and diverse genres, the Halifax Jazz Festival has become a highlight of the city's cultural calendar.

The festival takes place in various venues across Halifax, transforming the city into a dynamic hub of musical performances. From intimate jazz clubs to open-air stages, the festival offers a diverse range of settings where the sounds of jazz, blues, funk, and soul fill the air. Whether you're a devoted jazz aficionado or simply someone who appreciates the power of live music, the Halifax Jazz Festival promises an electrifying atmosphere that is sure to captivate and inspire.

One of the festival's main draws is its lineup of internationally renowned jazz artists who grace the stages with their exceptional talent. From Grammy Award winners to emerging stars, the festival consistently attracts some of the most esteemed musicians in the genre. Audiences have the opportunity to witness virtuosic performances and experience the magic of live improvisation as these artists showcase their artistry and push the boundaries of jazz.

In addition to the headlining acts, the Halifax Jazz Festival also shines a spotlight on the local music scene, providing a platform for talented musicians from the region to showcase their skills. Halifax has a vibrant and diverse music community, and the festival serves as a showcase for the city's wealth of talent. From up-and-coming jazz ensembles to established local favorites, these performances demonstrate the city's creative spirit and contribute to the festival's unique atmosphere.

The festival's programming extends beyond traditional jazz, embracing a wide range of musical styles and influences. This inclusive approach ensures that there is something for everyone, regardless of their musical preferences. Whether you find yourself captivated by the soulful melodies of a jazz quartet, grooving to the infectious rhythms of a funk ensemble, or getting lost in the bluesy notes of a talented guitarist, the Halifax Jazz Festival delivers a diverse and exciting musical experience.

Beyond the captivating performances, the festival offers an immersive atmosphere that encourages interaction and community engagement. In addition to the main stage performances, attendees can enjoy smaller, more intimate shows, workshops, and jam sessions that take place in local venues and jazz clubs throughout the city. These intimate settings provide a unique opportunity to get up close and personal with the musicians, fostering a sense of connection and appreciation for the art form.

The Halifax Jazz Festival is not just about the music; it's also a celebration of the city's cultural heritage and artistic expression. Throughout the festival, attendees can explore the various food vendors, artisans, and cultural displays that contribute to the vibrant atmosphere. The festival's location in downtown Halifax allows visitors to discover the city's rich history, explore its eclectic shops and eateries, and soak in the charming maritime ambiance that makes Halifax such a unique destination.

For those who want to actively participate, the Halifax Jazz Festival offers workshops and educational programs that cater to aspiring musicians, jazz enthusiasts, and curious learners of all ages. These workshops provide a valuable opportunity to learn from seasoned professionals, hone your musical skills, and gain insight into the creative process behind jazz and related genres. Whether you're a beginner looking to develop your musical abilities or a seasoned musician seeking to refine your craft, these educational offerings add an enriching dimension to the festival experience.

In summary, the Halifax Jazz Festival is a musical extravaganza that showcases the best of jazz and related genres. With its diverse lineup, world-class performances, and infectious energy, the festival has earned a reputation as one of the premier jazz events in Canada. Whether you're a dedicated jazz fan or simply looking for an unforgettable musical experience, the Halifax Jazz Festival offers an immersive and electrifying atmosphere where you can dance, groove, and revel in the magic of live music. Come and be a part of this celebration of music, culture, and community in the heart of Halifax.

Halifax Citadel National Historic Site: Reliving Military History

Step back in time at the Halifax Citadel National Historic Site, a star-shaped fortress that overlooks the city of Halifax. This magnificent structure stands as a testament to Halifax's military past and offers visitors a unique opportunity to delve into the history and heritage of the region. As you explore the fortifications, ramparts, and barracks, you'll be transported to the 19th-century and witness the daily life of soldiers through the expertise of costumed interpreters.

The Halifax Citadel, also known as Fort George, was constructed between 1828 and 1856 to defend the city and its valuable harbor. Its strategic location atop Citadel Hill provided an ideal vantage point to protect against potential attacks. The fortress was designed in the shape of a star, a popular architectural form for military defenses of that era. Today, the Halifax Citadel stands as one of the best-preserved examples of a 19th-century British fortification in North America.

Upon entering the Halifax Citadel National Historic Site, visitors are greeted by knowledgeable guides dressed in period uniforms. These costumed interpreters breathe life into the past, portraying soldiers and officers who once served at the Citadel. Their attention to historical accuracy and their ability to convey the experiences of those who lived and worked within the fortress truly make the visit an immersive and educational journey.

As you explore the site, you'll have the opportunity to roam through the various areas of the Citadel. Walk along the ramparts, where soldiers once stood watch, and enjoy panoramic views of the city, harbor, and surrounding landscape. The fortifications, with their thick stone walls and strategically placed cannons, evoke a sense of the Citadel's defensive purpose.

Inside the barracks, you'll step into the soldiers' living quarters, where the daily routines and challenges of military life come alive. Costumed interpreters will explain the soldiers' daily activities, the training they underwent, and the equipment and uniforms they used. You might witness the drilling and musket-firing demonstrations, providing an authentic glimpse into the rigorous training and discipline required of the soldiers.

One of the most iconic experiences at the Halifax Citadel is the firing of the Noon Gun. At precisely 12:00 noon, a cannon is fired, echoing across the city and signaling midday. This tradition has been faithfully upheld for over 150 years and continues to be a daily spectacle that draws locals and visitors alike. Witnessing the firing of the Noon Gun is not only a captivating event but also a connection to the Citadel's past and an opportunity to participate in a living historical tradition.

Beyond the physical structures and demonstrations, the Halifax Citadel National Historic Site offers a wealth of educational exhibits and displays. The on-site museum houses a collection of artifacts, uniforms, and weaponry from the 19th century, shedding light on the lives of the soldiers and the historical context in which they operated. Interactive exhibits engage visitors of all ages, allowing them to touch historical objects and further immerse themselves in the fascinating world of the past.

Guided tours and interpretive programs are available throughout the day, providing in-depth insights into the strategic importance of Halifax, its role in the British

Empire, and the daily lives of the soldiers stationed at the Citadel. Knowledgeable guides share captivating stories and anecdotes, painting a vivid picture of the challenges and triumphs experienced within these stone walls.

In addition to its historical significance, the Halifax Citadel National Historic Site also serves as a venue for various events and reenactments. Throughout the year, visitors may have the opportunity to witness military drills, music performances, and special ceremonies that evoke the atmosphere of the 19th century. These events add an extra layer of authenticity and excitement to the visitor experience, offering a glimpse into the past that is both educational and entertaining.

Visiting the Halifax Citadel National Historic Site is not only an opportunity to learn about the military history of the region but also a chance to appreciate the stunning architecture and breathtaking views it offers. The panoramic vistas from the ramparts allow you to admire the cityscape, the bustling harbor, and the vast expanse of the Atlantic Ocean. The juxtaposition of the ancient stone fortifications against the backdrop of a modern cityscape is a sight to behold and offers a unique perspective on Halifax's evolution over time.

As you explore the Halifax Citadel National Historic Site, you'll find yourself transported back to an era of military discipline, strategic fortifications, and a rich historical legacy. Through the immersive experiences, knowledgeable interpreters, and engaging exhibits, you'll gain a deep appreciation for the significance of the Halifax Citadel and the role it played in shaping the history of the city and the region. Whether you're a history enthusiast, a curious traveler, or simply someone seeking a memorable experience, a visit to the Halifax Citadel is sure to leave a lasting impression and a newfound understanding of Halifax's military heritage.

Halifax International Busker Festival: Street Performances and Entertainment

Join the lively crowds at the Halifax International Busker Festival, an annual event that transforms the city into a vibrant stage for street performers from around the world. With its captivating performances, lively atmosphere, and diverse range of acts, the festival has become a beloved highlight on Halifax's cultural calendar. For several days each summer, the streets of downtown Halifax come alive with the sights and sounds of talented buskers showcasing their skills and entertaining audiences of all ages.

The Halifax International Busker Festival has a rich history that dates back to its inception in 1986. Originally a small gathering of local street performers, the festival has grown exponentially over the years, attracting renowned buskers from various countries. Today, it is one of the largest and most prestigious busker festivals in North America, drawing both locals and tourists who come to witness the extraordinary talent on display.

One of the defining characteristics of the festival is the incredible variety of acts it offers. From awe-inspiring acrobatics to mind-boggling magic tricks, and from hilarious comedy routines to mesmerizing circus performances, there is something for everyone. As you stroll through the festival grounds, you'll encounter performers with diverse skills and backgrounds, each offering their own unique form of entertainment.

The festival's acrobats never fail to leave audiences in awe with their daring feats of strength, balance, and agility. Witness breathtaking aerial displays as performers gracefully soar through the air on trapezes and silks, defying gravity with seemingly effortless movements. Marvel at the heart-stopping stunts performed on towering stacks of chairs or by fearless fire jugglers who manipulate flames with mesmerizing precision. These acrobatic acts are a testament to the sheer talent and dedication of the performers who push the boundaries of what is physically possible.

Laughter fills the air as hilarious comedians take to the festival's stages, using their quick wit and engaging personalities to entertain and engage with the audience. With their clever wordplay, improvisational skills, and comedic timing, these talented performers create an atmosphere of joy and merriment. Whether it's a slapstick routine, a witty stand-up set, or interactive comedic magic, the comedians at the Halifax International Busker Festival have a knack for tickling funny bones and spreading contagious laughter throughout the crowd.

Circus acts are another highlight of the festival, captivating audiences with their awe-inspiring displays of skill and showmanship. From graceful aerial silk performances to jaw-dropping contortion routines, and from mesmerizing hoop tricks to gravity-defying hand-balancing acts, circus performers bring a sense of wonder and enchantment to the festival. Their carefully choreographed routines, often accompanied by vibrant costumes and captivating music, transport spectators to a world of fantasy and make-believe.

One of the remarkable aspects of the Halifax International Busker Festival is its ability to cater to audiences of all ages. Families can enjoy a day of wholesome entertainment as they watch family-friendly acts that combine comedy, acrobatics, and magic tricks. Children's faces light up with delight as they interact with the performers, and parents appreciate the festival's commitment to providing a safe and inclusive environment for everyone.

Beyond the mesmerizing performances, the festival also offers a bustling marketplace where visitors can browse a wide array of artisanal crafts, unique souvenirs, and delectable treats. Local vendors set up stalls, showcasing their handcrafted goods, artwork, and delicious food offerings. It's a wonderful opportunity to support local artisans and take home a memento that captures the spirit of the festival and Halifax's vibrant arts and culture scene.

The Halifax International Busker Festival is more than just a series of performances; it's an experience that immerses visitors in a world of imagination and creativity. The festival's joyful and energetic atmosphere is infectious, drawing people from all walks of life to come together and celebrate the power of street performance. It fosters a sense of community and camaraderie, with strangers bonding over shared moments of awe, laughter, and applause.

For both performers and audiences, the festival is a unique platform for artistic expression and cultural exchange. It provides a space for buskers to showcase their talents to an appreciative audience and for spectators to engage with diverse forms of entertainment from around the world. The festival's international flavor is a testament to the universal language of performance, breaking down barriers and fostering connections between people of different cultures and backgrounds.

The Halifax International Busker Festival has become an integral part of Halifax's identity, reflecting the city's vibrant arts and cultural scene. Its enduring popularity and continued growth are a testament to the festival's ability to captivate and inspire. Year after year, it draws thousands of visitors who eagerly await the chance to witness the extraordinary talent that graces its stages.

Whether you find yourself amazed by jaw-dropping acrobatics, laughing uncontrollably at hilarious comedians, or marveling at mesmerizing circus acts, the Halifax International Busker Festival promises an unforgettable experience. Join the lively crowds, immerse yourself in the joyful atmosphere, and let the festival's unique blend of entertainment ignite your sense of wonder and appreciation for the performing arts.

Exploring the Waterfront: Seafaring Heritage and Modern Attractions

Halifax Waterfront Boardwalk: Strolling Along the Harbor

The Halifax Waterfront Boardwalk is an iconic feature of the city, renowned for its scenic beauty and vibrant atmosphere. Stretching along the harbor, this picturesque promenade offers visitors an enchanting experience as they stroll along the water's edge, taking in the stunning views that unfold before them. The boardwalk serves as a bustling hub of activity, teeming with locals and tourists alike, all drawn to its charms.

As you embark on your journey along the Halifax Waterfront Boardwalk, you'll find yourself immersed in a sensory delight. The invigorating scent of the ocean fills the air, mingling with the aroma of freshly brewed coffee and delectable treats emanating from the nearby cafes and bakeries. The sound of seagulls overhead and the gentle lapping of the waves against the docks create a soothing backdrop, inviting you to slow down and savor the moment.

Lined with an array of charming shops, the boardwalk beckons you to explore their treasures. Here, you'll find a diverse range of boutiques and souvenir stores, offering everything from locally crafted jewelry and artwork to unique maritime-themed gifts. Browse through the collection of handmade goods, immerse yourself in the creativity of local artisans, and find the perfect memento to commemorate your visit to Halifax.

As you continue your leisurely stroll, the boardwalk reveals its historical significance. Along the way, you'll encounter landmarks that tell tales of Halifax's past. Stop by the Historic Properties, a collection of beautifully restored buildings that date back to the 18th century, and marvel at their architectural splendor. These heritage structures now house a variety of shops, galleries, and restaurants, seamlessly blending the old with the new.

One of the highlights of the Halifax Waterfront Boardwalk is the sight of magnificent vessels dotting the harbor. Tall ships with their towering masts, fishing boats unloading their fresh catch, and luxurious yachts create a captivating maritime scene. The maritime industry has long been intertwined with Halifax's identity, and this bustling harbor pays homage to that seafaring heritage. Take a moment to appreciate the craftsmanship and the stories behind these vessels as you observe them in their natural element.

The boardwalk is also alive with entertainment, thanks to the talented street performers who fill the air with music, laughter, and applause. From musicians strumming their guitars to magicians mesmerizing the crowd, their performances add an extra layer of charm to your waterfront experience. Pause for a while, allow yourself to be captivated by their talents, and perhaps even join in the joyful atmosphere by tossing a few coins into their collection hats.

When hunger strikes, the Halifax Waterfront Boardwalk offers an abundance of culinary delights to satisfy your palate. From casual eateries serving up the freshest seafood to upscale restaurants showcasing innovative cuisine, there's something to please every taste. Indulge in a classic lobster roll, savor the delicate flavors of freshly shucked oysters, or treat yourself to a piping hot bowl of seafood chowder. As you dine, let the mesmerizing waterfront views accompany your meal, enhancing the sensory experience.

The Halifax Waterfront Boardwalk is not merely a place to pass through but a destination in itself. It's a place to unwind, to connect with the city's maritime spirit, and to embrace the vibrant energy that flows through its veins. Whether you're a history buff, a food lover, an art enthusiast, or simply seeking a leisurely stroll, the boardwalk caters to all.

In the summer months, the boardwalk comes alive with festivals and events, drawing crowds from near and far. From the Halifax Jazz Festival, where the waterfront becomes a stage for world-class musicians, to the Tall Ships Festival, where majestic vessels from around the globe gather, these celebrations add an extra layer of excitement to your visit. Immerse yourself in the maritime festivities, dance to the rhythms of live music, and witness the spectacle of illuminated boats parading along the harbor during the annual holiday boat parade.

Whether you visit the Halifax Waterfront Boardwalk during the lively summer months or in the quieter seasons when a sense of tranquility permeates the air, it never fails to leave a lasting impression. The blend of natural beauty, historical significance, cultural vibrancy, and culinary delights creates an experience that is uniquely Halifax. So, take your time, savor every step, and let the Halifax Waterfront Boardwalk weave its magic as you explore the city's captivating waterfront.

Canadian Museum of Immigration at Pier 21: Stories of New Beginnings

Located on the picturesque waterfront of Halifax, the Canadian Museum of Immigration at Pier 21 serves as a powerful testament to Canada's vibrant immigration history and the incredible stories of those who arrived on its shores in search of new beginnings. The museum's location at Pier 21, often referred to as the "Gateway to Canada," holds significant historical and cultural importance, as it was the primary point of entry for over one million immigrants between 1928 and 1971.

Stepping into the museum is like embarking on a captivating journey through time. Visitors are greeted by a warm and inviting atmosphere, where interactive exhibits, personal accounts, and authentic artifacts combine to tell the compelling tales of immigrants who passed through Pier 21. The museum's mission is to shed light on the challenges, triumphs, and cultural contributions of immigrants from around the world, fostering a deeper understanding of Canada's multicultural fabric and the profound impact of immigration on the nation's identity.

As you delve into the exhibits, you'll find yourself immersed in the personal narratives of individuals and families who left their homelands behind and embarked on a courageous journey to a new life in Canada. Their stories come to life through audio recordings, photographs, and written testimonies, offering a poignant glimpse into the hopes, dreams, and struggles they faced along the way. From war-torn countries seeking refuge to individuals seeking economic opportunities, each story represents a unique chapter in Canada's immigration narrative.

The museum's exhibits are thoughtfully curated, providing visitors with a comprehensive understanding of the immigration process and its profound impact on Canadian society. One exhibit, titled "Arrival," recreates the bustling atmosphere of Pier 21, allowing visitors to experience the anticipation and emotions felt by newcomers as they arrived on Canadian soil. Authentic luggage, uniforms, and personal belongings on display serve as tangible reminders of the sacrifices made and the cherished possessions that accompanied individuals on their journey.

Moving through the museum, you'll encounter the "Departures" exhibit, which explores the motivations that led people to leave their homelands and the often heartbreaking farewells they said to loved ones. This section delves into the push and pull factors that influenced migration, such as political unrest, economic hardship, and the promise of a better life in Canada. It highlights the diverse range of cultures and countries represented by the immigrants who chose to make Canada their new home.

The "Settlement" exhibit takes visitors on a step-by-step journey through the early days of immigration, exploring the challenges faced by newcomers as they adjusted to life in an unfamiliar land. Through immersive displays, you'll witness the efforts made by immigrants to build communities, establish businesses, and preserve their cultural heritage while adapting to the Canadian way of life. The exhibit underscores the resilience and determination of immigrants who contributed significantly to the growth and development of their adopted country.

One of the most powerful aspects of the Canadian Museum of Immigration at Pier 21 is its emphasis on the human stories that lie at the heart of the immigration experience. Personal accounts shared through video interviews and interactive displays bring the past to life, creating an emotional connection between visitors and the individuals whose lives were forever changed by their decision to come to Canada. These stories transcend time, reminding us of the shared humanity and the collective strength found in diversity.

Additionally, the museum recognizes that immigration is an ongoing process, and its exhibits extend beyond historical narratives to include contemporary immigration experiences. By showcasing the contributions of recent immigrants and exploring the issues and challenges faced by newcomers today, the museum creates a bridge between the past and the present, fostering dialogue and understanding.

The Canadian Museum of Immigration at Pier 21 offers a range of educational programs and activities designed to engage visitors of all ages. Guided tours, workshops, and interactive exhibits provide opportunities for deeper exploration and reflection. The museum's dedication to preserving and sharing Canada's immigration history has garnered international recognition, making it a significant cultural institution and a must-visit destination for those interested in understanding the roots of Canada's diverse society.

In conclusion, the Canadian Museum of Immigration at Pier 21 stands as a living tribute to the millions of immigrants who have shaped Canada's identity and contributed to its cultural mosaic. By exploring the interactive exhibits, personal accounts, and artifacts that fill its halls, visitors gain a profound appreciation for the immense courage, resilience, and tenacity displayed by individuals and families who embarked on the challenging journey to a new life in Canada. The museum serves as a reminder of the transformative power of immigration and the enduring legacy left by those who sought refuge, opportunity, and a place to call home on Canadian soil.

Theodore Tugboat: A Maritime Adventure for Kids

For young maritime enthusiasts, a visit to Theodore Tugboat in Halifax is an absolute must. Inspired by the beloved children's television show, Theodore Tugboat brings the animated characters to life in a captivating real-world setting. This unique maritime adventure allows children to embark on a journey aboard a charming replica of Theodore, the friendly and adventurous tugboat, as they set sail on the harbor waters of Halifax.

As soon as children step aboard Theodore Tugboat, they are greeted with an atmosphere of excitement and anticipation. The colorful and vibrant interior of the tugboat instantly captures their imagination, transporting them into the world of the beloved television series. The attention to detail in recreating Theodore's appearance is remarkable, from his cheery smile to his bright red color that symbolizes his enthusiasm for life on the water.

The experience aboard Theodore Tugboat is not only entertaining but also educational, providing a unique opportunity for children to learn about maritime navigation and the importance of teamwork on the water. Through interactive activities and engaging storytelling, young visitors gain insights into the daily tasks and responsibilities of a tugboat crew. They can participate in hands-on experiences that simulate steering the tugboat, operating the controls, and learning basic navigation techniques. These activities not only spark their curiosity but also foster an appreciation for the maritime industry and the important role tugboats play in supporting maritime operations.

One of the highlights of the Theodore Tugboat experience is the chance to meet other characters from the television series. From Hank the Barge to George the Valiant, each character has their own unique personality and contributes to the dynamic world of the harbor. Meeting these beloved characters in person adds an extra layer of excitement and joy to the visit, creating cherished memories that children will treasure for years to come.

Throughout the journey, experienced and friendly guides share fascinating stories and anecdotes about the harbor, its history, and the maritime activities that take place on its waters. Children are encouraged to ask questions, satisfying their curiosity and deepening their understanding of Halifax's seafaring culture. The guides are passionate about their work and are skilled at captivating the attention of young audiences, ensuring an engaging and enriching experience for everyone on board.

As Theodore Tugboat sails along the harbor waters, children have the opportunity to observe the bustling maritime activity around them. They can witness large ships docking and unloading cargo, see smaller boats navigating the waterways, and even catch a glimpse of marine wildlife that call the harbor home. This firsthand exposure to the maritime environment fosters a sense of connection and appreciation for the coastal city of Halifax and its unique seafaring heritage.

Theodore Tugboat not only caters to individual visitors but also offers special programs and events for schools and organized groups. These educational outings provide an interactive and memorable experience for students, complementing their classroom learning with a hands-on exploration of maritime concepts. Students can apply their knowledge of navigation, geography, and teamwork in a practical and engaging manner, making the experience both fun and educational.

Beyond its educational value, Theodore Tugboat also serves as a symbol of friendship, teamwork, and kindness – themes that are prominently featured in the television series. Through the adventures of Theodore and his friends, children learn the importance of helping others, being inclusive, and embracing diversity. The experience aboard Theodore Tugboat reinforces these positive values, nurturing the development of empathy, compassion, and social skills in young visitors.

Theodore Tugboat has become an iconic attraction in Halifax, beloved by both locals and visitors alike. Its enduring popularity is a testament to the show's impact on generations of children and its ability to bring maritime adventures to life. The experience of sailing on Theodore Tugboat creates lasting memories, ignites a sense of wonder, and inspires children to explore the world around them with curiosity and enthusiasm.

In conclusion, Theodore Tugboat offers young maritime enthusiasts a delightful and immersive experience that combines entertainment with education. Inspired by the beloved children's television show, this real-world maritime adventure allows children to set sail on the harbor waters of

Halifax aboard a charming replica of Theodore Tugboat. Through interactive activities, engaging storytelling, and the opportunity to meet other characters from the show, children can immerse themselves in Halifax's seafaring culture while learning about maritime navigation and teamwork. The experience aboard Theodore Tugboat fosters a love for the sea, nurtures curiosity, and creates cherished memories that will last a lifetime.

Tall Ships: Sailing Ships and Maritime Festivities

Halifax has a long-standing connection to tall ships, and the city regularly hosts majestic vessels from around the world during tall ship festivals and events. Marvel at the grandeur of these magnificent sailing ships as they dock along the waterfront, their masts reaching for the sky. Take the opportunity to step aboard and explore these stunning vessels, learning about their rich history and the art of traditional seamanship. During tall ship festivals, the waterfront comes alive with music, performances, and maritime-themed activities, offering a Halifax, with its deep-rooted maritime heritage, has fostered a long-standing connection with tall ships, becoming a magnet for majestic vessels from around the world. Visitors to the city have the unique opportunity to witness the grandeur of these magnificent sailing ships as they grace the waterfront during tall ship festivals and events. These events provide an immersive experience that transports visitors back in time and allows them to appreciate the rich history and art of traditional seamanship.

As the tall ships dock along the Halifax waterfront, an awe-inspiring sight unfolds. Their towering masts, adorned with billowing sails, reach towards the sky, casting a majestic silhouette against the horizon. The ships themselves are a testament to the intricate craftsmanship and engineering marvels of the past. Each vessel has a unique story to tell, representing different eras and styles of sailing.

Stepping aboard one of these tall ships is akin to entering a living museum. The decks creak underfoot, and the scent of saltwater fills the air, instantly transporting visitors to a bygone era of maritime exploration. Experienced crew members, dressed in period costumes, are on hand to share their knowledge and passion for the ship and its history. Visitors can explore the various parts of the vessel, from the commanding bridge to the cozy quarters below deck. They can marvel at the intricate rigging, walk along the weathered planks, and imagine the challenges faced by sailors who braved the open seas.

One of the highlights of the tall ship festivals is the opportunity to engage with the crew and learn about the rich history and traditions of these seafaring vessels. The crew members are often eager to share tales of daring voyages, explain the intricacies of navigation, and demonstrate the techniques of traditional seamanship. Visitors can gain a deeper appreciation for the skills and courage required to navigate these majestic ships across vast oceans.

During these festivals, the Halifax waterfront comes alive with a vibrant celebration of Halifax's seafaring heritage. The air is filled with the sounds of music and laughter as live performances and maritime-themed activities take center stage. Local musicians entertain the crowds with lively sea shanties and traditional folk tunes, adding to the festive atmosphere. Artists and artisans showcase their talents, displaying maritime-themed artworks and handcrafted treasures.

Visitors can participate in interactive workshops, where they can learn the basics of knot tying, try their hand at maritime crafts, or even have a go at steering a ship simulator. Maritime history enthusiasts will find themselves immersed in educational exhibits that highlight Halifax's significance as a port city and its role in naval operations. These exhibits often feature artifacts from notable shipwrecks, displays of navigational instruments, and informative panels detailing Halifax's maritime legacy.

The tall ship festivals also offer an array of culinary delights for visitors to savor. Food vendors line the waterfront, offering a delectable selection of seafood specialties and local delicacies. From succulent lobster rolls to freshly shucked oysters, visitors can indulge in the flavors of the sea while enjoying the bustling ambiance of the festival. The tantalizing aroma of freshly cooked seafood mingles with the salty breeze, creating an irresistible invitation to sample the maritime culinary treasures of Halifax.

For families, the tall ship festivals provide a captivating experience for children of all ages. Kids can embark on their own maritime adventure as they explore the decks of the tall ships and interact with the crew. The crews often have special activities and programs designed to engage young visitors, fostering a sense of wonder and curiosity about the seafaring world. One highlight for children is the chance to participate in the daily routines of life on board a tall ship, from hoisting flags to learning basic seamanship skills.

The tall ship festivals in Halifax are not just limited to the vessels themselves. Spectacular parades of sail take place as the ships navigate through the harbor, creating a breathtaking spectacle for onlookers. The sight of these majestic vessels, gracefully maneuvering under sail, evokes a sense of awe and admiration for the skills of the sailors and the beauty of the ships. The parade of sail is a favorite among photographers and maritime enthusiasts, providing a memorable and picturesque experience.

As the sun sets over the Halifax waterfront, the tall ship festivals take on a magical ambiance. The ships are illuminated, casting a soft glow across the harbor, creating a scene reminiscent of a bygone era. Visitors can enjoy evening concerts, fireworks displays, and even evening sails on some of the tall ships. The shimmering lights reflecting on the water, combined with the enchanting melodies and maritime-themed performances, create a truly unforgettable experience.

For both locals and visitors, the tall ship festivals in Halifax offer a captivating blend of history, entertainment, and celebration. They provide a window into the city's seafaring past, honoring its rich maritime heritage and the resilience of those who sailed the seas. Whether exploring the decks of these magnificent vessels, engaging with the crew, or simply immersing oneself in the festive atmosphere, the tall ship festivals in Halifax are an experience that truly brings the magic of maritime festivities to life.

Halifax Seaport Farmers' Market: Culinary Delights and Local Flavors

Nestled along the picturesque waterfront, the Halifax Seaport Farmers' Market stands as a culinary haven and a vibrant gathering place for food enthusiasts. With a history dating back over two centuries, it proudly holds the title of the oldest continuously operating farmers' market in North America. Stepping into this bustling marketplace is like entering a world of delectable aromas, colorful displays, and the warm embrace of community.

As you wander through the market stalls, your senses are immediately captivated by the sights, sounds, and smells. Local farmers proudly display their freshly harvested produce, bursting with vibrant colors and flavors. From plump heirloom tomatoes and crisp greens to juicy berries and fragrant herbs, the market showcases the region's bountiful harvest. It's a treasure trove of seasonal delights, offering a true farm-to-table experience.

Beyond the colorful fruits and vegetables, the market entices with an enticing array of artisanal products. Skilled bakers tempt you with their oven-fresh bread, flaky pastries, and decadent desserts. Cheesemakers showcase their carefully crafted cheeses, from creamy camemberts to tangy cheddars, each with its own distinctive character. Local beekeepers offer jars of golden honey, while chocolatiers showcase their handcrafted treats. The market is a paradise for food lovers, where every corner reveals a new culinary delight.

But the Halifax Seaport Farmers' Market is more than just a place to indulge in exceptional food—it's a vibrant community gathering place. Locals and visitors alike converge here to share their love for food, connect with artisans and farmers, and celebrate the region's flavors. The lively atmosphere is filled with laughter, conversation, and the joy of discovery. Families gather to shop for the week's groceries, friends catch up over a cup of freshly brewed coffee, and tourists immerse themselves in the local culture.

One of the highlights of the market experience is the opportunity to savor a mouthwatering brunch or a quick bite amidst the vibrant ambiance. Local vendors and food stalls offer an enticing variety of options. Treat yourself to a fluffy stack of pancakes drizzled with maple syrup from nearby sugar shacks. Sample a warm and savory breakfast sandwich made with free-range eggs and locally sourced bacon. Or opt for a hearty bowl of homemade soup, prepared with farm-fresh ingredients and served alongside freshly baked bread. Whether you're a fan of sweet or savory, vegetarian or carnivorous, the market has something to satisfy every palate.

As you navigate the market's lively aisles, you'll also find an assortment of non-food offerings. Local artisans showcase their handmade crafts, including jewelry, pottery, textiles, and artwork. It's a wonderful opportunity to find unique souvenirs, one-of-a-kind gifts, or even adorn yourself with a piece of locally crafted jewelry. The market fosters a sense of community support and appreciation for local talent, making it a hub of creativity and entrepreneurship.

During the warmer months, the market spills out onto the waterfront, creating a vibrant outdoor space. Visitors can gather at communal tables, basking in the sunshine while enjoying their market finds. The nearby harbor serves as a picturesque backdrop, providing a serene atmosphere for a leisurely picnic. Grab a selection of fresh fruits, artisanal cheeses, and crusty bread, and create your own al fresco feast while watching sailboats glide across the shimmering waters.

Throughout the year, the market hosts special events and themed festivals that further showcase the region's culinary diversity. From seafood extravaganzas to celebrations of local harvests, these events offer an immersive experience where visitors can engage with local chefs, farmers, and food artisans. It's a chance to learn about traditional cooking techniques, discover new flavors, and deepen your appreciation for the region's gastronomic heritage.

For those seeking a deeper connection to the local food scene, the market provides opportunities to engage with farmers directly. Conversations with growers offer insights into sustainable farming practices, seasonal produce, and the challenges and joys of cultivating the land. As you connect with the people behind the food, you gain a deeper understanding of the commitment to quality and the passion that goes into each product.

Visiting the Halifax Seaport Farmers' Market is not just about indulging in delicious food and discovering unique crafts—it's an experience that nourishes both the body and the soul. It's a place where the community comes together, forging connections, and celebrating the region's flavors. Whether you're a food lover, a curious traveler, or simply someone looking to immerse yourself in the local culture, the market offers a vibrant and memorable experience that will leave you with a deeper appreciation for Halifax's culinary heritage.

Outdoor Adventures: Embracing Halifax's Natural Beauty

Halifax offers an abundance of outdoor adventures that allow visitors to immerse themselves in the city's stunning natural beauty. From urban oases to untouched wilderness, here are some remarkable outdoor attractions that are sure to captivate nature enthusiasts:

Point Pleasant Park: Urban Oasis with Scenic Trails

Nestled at the southern tip of the Halifax Peninsula, Point Pleasant Park stands as a tranquil urban oasis, offering visitors a much-needed escape from the bustling city. Spanning over 75 hectares, this historic park showcases the region's natural beauty with its diverse landscapes, scenic trails, and captivating vistas. As you step foot into Point Pleasant Park, you are immediately greeted by a sense of tranquility and serenity.

The park's network of scenic trails is a haven for outdoor enthusiasts and nature lovers alike. Whether you prefer leisurely walks, invigorating jogs, or cycling adventures, Point Pleasant Park has something to offer for everyone. As you meander along the winding paths, you'll be treated to breathtaking views of the vast Atlantic Ocean, where the horizon merges with the endless sky, creating a sense of limitless possibilities. The rhythmic sound of crashing waves provides a soothing backdrop as you explore the park's picturesque coves and hidden alcoves.

The lush forests that blanket Point Pleasant Park offer a refuge for both flora and fauna. Tall, majestic trees create a verdant canopy, providing shade and shelter for numerous species of birds and small mammals. As you wander through the forested trails, you may catch glimpses of colorful songbirds flitting from branch to branch or squirrels playfully scampering along the forest floor. The park's biodiversity showcases the delicate balance of nature and reminds us of the importance of preserving these natural habitats.

Point Pleasant Park holds a special place in Halifax's history, and its grounds are peppered with several historic landmarks that tell stories of the past. One such iconic landmark is the Prince of Wales Tower, a stone fortification that dates back to the 18th century. This National Historic Site stands as a testament to Halifax's strategic importance in protecting the region from potential threats. As you explore the tower, you can imagine the soldiers who once stood guard within its walls, protecting the city's interests and heritage.

In addition to the Prince of Wales Tower, Point Pleasant Park boasts other notable landmarks and memorials that pay homage to Halifax's past. The Sailors' Memorial commemorates the sailors who lost their lives at sea, while the Martello Tower provides a glimpse into the city's military history. These landmarks serve as poignant reminders of the sacrifices made and the resilience of the people who have called Halifax home.

One of the unique features of Point Pleasant Park is its ability to cater to different preferences and interests. For those seeking moments of quiet reflection, the park offers numerous peaceful spots where you can sit, relax, and let the world fade away. Find a cozy bench overlooking the ocean, listen to the gentle rustle of leaves in the wind, and feel a sense of inner calm wash over you. The park's serene ambiance invites introspection and rejuvenation, providing a much-needed respite from the demands of daily life.

Beyond its natural beauty and historic significance, Point Pleasant Park also serves as a gathering place for the local community. Families come together for picnics on the grassy expanses, friends engage in lively conversations during leisurely walks, and joggers set their own pace as they navigate the park's trails. The park becomes a shared space, where people from all walks of life can connect with nature and with each other.

As the seasons change, so does the allure of Point Pleasant Park. In the spring, vibrant blossoms paint the landscape with a kaleidoscope of colors, while in the summer, the park becomes a lush, green sanctuary offering shade and cool breezes. In the fall, the foliage transforms into a symphony of reds, oranges, and yellows, creating a picturesque backdrop for leisurely strolls. Even in the winter, Point Pleasant Park has its own unique charm, with frosted trees and peaceful snowy trails inviting visitors to embrace the beauty of the season.

Point Pleasant Park is not merely a park; it's a sanctuary that encapsulates the essence of Halifax. It represents the city's commitment to preserving its natural heritage, celebrating its rich history, and providing a place for locals and visitors to forge connections with nature. Whether you seek solitude, a sense of adventure, or a deeper understanding of Halifax's past, Point Pleasant Park invites you to embark on a journey of exploration and discovery.

Peggy's Cove: A Quaint Fishing Village and Iconic Lighthouse

Located just a scenic drive from downtown Halifax, Peggy's Cove stands as a postcard-perfect fishing village that captivates visitors with its undeniable charm and breathtaking natural beauty. As one of Nova Scotia's most iconic destinations, Peggy's Cove offers a tranquil escape from the city, inviting travelers to immerse themselves in the simplicity and serenity of coastal living.

Nestled along the rugged shores of St. Margaret's Bay, Peggy's Cove is instantly recognizable for its famous landmark, the Peggy's Point Lighthouse. Perched atop weathered granite boulders, the lighthouse stands as a sentinel overlooking the picturesque harbor, guiding ships and capturing the imagination of all who lay eyes upon it. With its distinct red and white exterior, the lighthouse serves as an enduring symbol of maritime heritage and has become an emblem of Peggy's Cove itself.

Stepping into the village is like entering a time capsule, where the pace of life slows down and the essence of traditional fishing communities is preserved. The sight of colorful houses, their vibrant hues harmonizing with the surrounding natural beauty, welcomes visitors and offers a warm invitation to explore further. Strolling through the narrow lanes, you'll encounter traditional fishing shacks that still serve as a reminder of the village's rich seafaring history.

As you meander through the village, be sure to visit the small craft co-op, where local artisans proudly display their creations. Here, you can find an array of handmade crafts, from intricate woodwork to pottery, jewelry, and vibrant paintings. It's a wonderful opportunity to support the local community and bring home a unique piece of Peggy's Cove as a lasting memento.

But it is the rugged shoreline that truly steals the show in Peggy's Cove. The sound of crashing waves against the granite rocks creates a symphony of nature's power, while the scent of saltwater permeates the air, heightening the senses. Take your time to explore the shoreline, walking along the uneven terrain as you marvel at the unique rock formations that have been sculpted by centuries of relentless waves. Each step unveils a new vista, offering a constant reminder of the awe-inspiring forces of nature.

As you navigate the shoreline, you may encounter "black rocks," a dark-hued geological marvel that contrasts starkly with the surrounding landscape. These massive rocks, smoothed and shaped by the relentless Atlantic Ocean, provide an intriguing backdrop against the crashing waves and open skies. Take a moment to pause and breathe in the tranquility of this idyllic coastal gem, allowing the sounds and sights of Peggy's Cove to leave an indelible mark on your soul.

For those seeking a deeper connection with the village's history, a visit to the William E. deGarthe Memorial Provincial Park is a must. This unique park is home to a striking sculpture created by artist William deGarthe, paying homage to the hardworking fishermen who have long called Peggy's Cove their home. The massive granite carving portrays a scene of fishermen and their families, serving as a testament to the village's enduring spirit and the resilience of its people.

While Peggy's Cove is undeniably captivating during the daylight hours, it possesses a different kind of magic as dusk descends. As the golden hues of the setting sun bathe the landscape, the village takes on an ethereal quality. The iconic lighthouse, silhouetted against the fiery sky, stands as a sentinel guarding the secrets of the sea. Witnessing the transition from day to night in Peggy's Cove is a truly enchanting experience, one that lingers in the memory long after the visit.

As you bid farewell to Peggy's Cove, take a moment to reflect on the beauty and simplicity of this coastal haven. Its picturesque landscapes, charming village life, and the enduring allure of the Peggy's Point Lighthouse create a tapestry of experiences that evoke a sense of wonder and appreciation for the natural world. Peggy's Cove, with its tranquil shores and timeless charm, serves as a reminder of the profound impact that nature and a close-knit community can have on the human spirit.

McNabs Island: Exploring an Untouched Wilderness

For those seeking an off-the-beaten-path adventure, McNabs Island offers an opportunity to explore a pristine and untouched wilderness just a short ferry ride from Halifax. This uninhabited island, situated at the entrance of Halifax Harbour, is a nature lover's paradise, boasting diverse ecosystems, sandy beaches, and enchanting woodlands. With its rich natural beauty and intriguing historical significance, McNabs Island captivates visitors with its charm and allure.

Upon stepping foot on McNabs Island, you'll immediately feel a sense of tranquility as you leave the hustle and bustle of the city behind. The island spans over 395 hectares and is home to a remarkable variety of habitats, including forests, marshes, meadows, and rocky shorelines. This diverse ecosystem provides a haven for a wide array of plant and animal species, making it a perfect destination for nature enthusiasts and avid birdwatchers.

One of the best ways to explore McNabs Island is by embarking on its scenic trails, which meander through its captivating landscapes. The island features approximately 22 kilometers of trails, each offering a unique perspective of its natural wonders. As you hike through the wooded areas, you'll be surrounded by towering trees, wildflowers, and the melodious songs of birds. The trails also provide opportunities for wildlife spotting, so keep your eyes peeled for white-tailed deer gracefully traversing the terrain or seals lounging along the shoreline.

Throughout your journey, be sure to venture off the beaten path to discover hidden coves and secluded beaches. McNabs Island boasts several pristine sandy beaches, where you can unwind, bask in the sun, and listen to the gentle lapping of the waves. Take a refreshing dip in the clear waters, explore the tidal pools teeming with marine life, or simply relish in the serenity of your surroundings.

Aside from its natural wonders, McNabs Island is also a place of historical significance. As you wander through the island, you'll come across remnants of old fortifications and historic sites that tell tales of its past. Fort McNab, a military fortification built in the late 19th century, stands as a testament to the island's strategic role in Halifax's defenses. Explore the fort's weathered walls, wander through the barracks, and imagine the stories of soldiers who once called this place home.

The island's history extends beyond military fortifications. The Oland Family Cemetery, located near the eastern shore, offers a glimpse into the island's connection with the prominent Oland brewing family. Pay your respects as you wander among the gravestones and contemplate the island's cultural heritage.

To fully appreciate the historical and ecological significance of McNabs Island, consider joining a guided tour. Knowledgeable guides will lead you through the island, sharing captivating stories and insights into its past and present. Learn about the Mi'kmaq Indigenous people's connection to the land, the island's use during World War II, and the efforts to preserve its natural beauty.

Camping enthusiasts can also extend their stay on McNabs Island by pitching a tent at the designated camping area. Spend the night under the starry sky, surrounded by the peaceful sounds of nature. Wake up to the soothing melodies of songbirds and relish in the breathtaking sunrise over the horizon. Camping on McNabs Island offers a unique opportunity to fully immerse yourself in the island's beauty and tranquility.

As with any adventure in nature, it is essential to respect and preserve the delicate ecosystems of McNabs Island. Leave no trace, follow designated trails, and adhere to any conservation guidelines in place. By doing so, you contribute to the ongoing preservation of this natural gem for future generations to enjoy.

McNabs Island is a captivating destination that seamlessly blends untouched wilderness with fascinating history. Whether you're hiking through its scenic trails, exploring hidden coves, or discovering remnants of old fortifications, this island beckons you to embark on a journey of exploration and wonder. Escape the hustle of the city and let McNabs Island envelop you in its natural beauty and serenity.

Whale Watching Tours: Encountering Majestic Marine Life

Embarking on a whale watching tour in Halifax is a truly unforgettable experience that allows visitors to witness the awe-inspiring beauty of these majestic marine creatures in their natural habitat. Halifax is renowned for its exceptional whale watching opportunities, attracting nature enthusiasts from around the world who yearn to get up close and personal with these magnificent creatures. With specially equipped vessels and knowledgeable guides, these tours provide a unique and educational adventure into the deep waters of the Atlantic Ocean.

As you embark on a whale watching tour in Halifax, you'll find yourself filled with anticipation and excitement. The journey begins as you board the comfortable and sturdy vessel, designed specifically for optimal wildlife viewing. These boats are equipped with observation decks, allowing for unobstructed views of the surrounding waters, and are built to minimize any disturbance to the marine life. Once the vessel sets sail, the experienced crew will navigate the waters in search of whales and other marine wildlife.

Halifax's waters are home to several whale species, with humpback whales and minke whales being among the most commonly sighted. These gentle giants of the sea captivate onlookers with their graceful movements and impressive size. The humpback whales, known for their acrobatic displays such as breaching and tail slapping, often steal the show. Witnessing their massive bodies launch out of the water or their tails crashing against the surface is a sight that leaves spectators in awe.

As you sail further into the Atlantic Ocean, you may also encounter pods of dolphins playfully riding the bow waves, exhibiting their agility and playful behavior. These intelligent creatures often accompany the boats, leaping in and out of the water, creating a sense of joy and wonder for all on board. Additionally, porpoises may make appearances, gliding gracefully through the water with their distinctive fin shapes.

One of the most remarkable aspects of a whale watching tour in Halifax is the presence of knowledgeable guides who are passionate about marine life. These experts provide valuable commentary throughout the excursion, sharing fascinating insights about the behavior, biology, and conservation efforts related to the whales and other marine species. They help passengers understand the importance of preserving these fragile ecosystems and emphasize the significance of responsible wildlife tourism.

During the tour, the guides will enlighten you about the whales' migration patterns, feeding habits, and social interactions. You'll learn about the incredible journeys these whales undertake, traveling thousands of kilometers each year between their feeding grounds and breeding areas. The guides may also educate you about the individual whales that frequent the region, sharing stories of their distinctive characteristics, such as unique tail patterns that help researchers identify and track them.

As you patiently scan the horizon, the anticipation builds with each passing moment. The guides will instruct you on what signs to look for, such as spouts of water, flukes breaking the surface, or the mesmerizing sight of a whale's back arching as it prepares for a deep dive. The atmosphere on the boat is filled with anticipation and excitement, as passengers eagerly keep their eyes peeled, ready to catch a glimpse of these magnificent creatures.

Finally, the moment arrives—a massive humpback whale breaches just meters away from the boat, its colossal body propelling out of the water before gracefully crashing back into the depths. The sheer power and grace of this natural spectacle leave you in awe, and a collective gasp of amazement ripples through the boat. Cameras click, capturing the precious moments as memories to be cherished forever.

Throughout the tour, the crew and guides maintain a respectful distance from the whales, ensuring the animals are not disturbed or endangered. They adhere to strict guidelines and regulations set in place to protect the marine life and their habitats. Responsible whale watching practices prioritize the well-being of the animals above all else, allowing visitors to appreciate their presence while minimizing any potential impact.

The experience of whale watching in Halifax is not limited to the captivating encounters with these magnificent creatures alone. The vastness of the Atlantic Ocean, the fresh ocean breeze against your face, and the sound of waves gently lapping against the hull create a serene and tranquil atmosphere. The tour itself becomes a voyage of discovery, immersing you in the beauty and serenity of the natural world.

As the tour draws to a close and the vessel heads back to shore, the memories of witnessing these majestic marine creatures up close will stay with you forever. The awe-inspiring beauty of the whales, the playful dolphins, and the educational insights provided by the guides combine to create an experience that is both breathtaking and enlightening. Whale watching tours in Halifax offer a unique opportunity to connect with nature, foster a deep appreciation for marine life, and inspire a commitment to their conservation.

In Halifax, where the pristine waters of the Atlantic Ocean meet the rugged coastline, whale watching becomes a profound and transformative experience. It serves as a reminder of the immense beauty that exists within our natural world and instills a sense of responsibility to protect and preserve these remarkable creatures for generations to come. A whale watching tour in Halifax is not just a mere excursion—it is an adventure that touches the heart and soul, leaving an indelible mark on all who have the privilege to participate.

Crystal Crescent Beach Provincial Park: Pristine Shorelines and Seaside Serenity

Located just a short drive from downtown Halifax, Crystal Crescent Beach Provincial Park is a true hidden gem nestled along the rugged coastline of Nova Scotia. This coastal park boasts three pristine white-sand beaches that beckon visitors with their natural beauty and serene ambiance. Offering a welcome respite from the city's hustle and bustle, Crystal Crescent Beach Provincial Park is the perfect destination for those seeking a tranquil escape and a chance to immerse themselves in the breathtaking scenery of the Atlantic Ocean.

As you approach the park, anticipation builds as glimpses of the sparkling turquoise waters and powdery white sands come into view. The first beach, aptly named First Beach, welcomes visitors with its wide expanse of soft sand and inviting waters. It is the most easily accessible beach, ideal for families and sun seekers looking to relax and soak up the sun. With its gentle slope and shallow waters, First Beach is also a popular spot for swimming and wading, providing a refreshing respite on hot summer days.

Venturing further along the park's picturesque shoreline, you'll reach Second Beach. This secluded crescent-shaped beach offers a more intimate and peaceful atmosphere, perfect for couples seeking a romantic stroll or individuals looking for solitude. As you sink your toes into the soft sand and listen to the soothing sound of the waves, you'll feel a sense of tranquility wash over you. The unspoiled beauty of Second Beach is truly a sight to behold, with its pristine sands stretching out before you and the vibrant hues of the ocean mesmerizing your senses.

Continuing your exploration, you'll discover the hidden gem of Third Beach. Tucked away from the main entrance, Third Beach offers a sense of seclusion and tranquility that is perfect for those seeking a more off-the-beaten-path experience. With its rugged shoreline and dramatic rock formations, this beach is a paradise for nature lovers and photographers alike. Capture the beauty of the crashing waves against the weathered rocks or take a leisurely walk along the beach, allowing the fresh ocean breeze to invigorate your senses.

Beyond the beaches, Crystal Crescent Beach Provincial Park also boasts a network of scenic trails that meander through the adjacent coastal barrens. These trails offer a chance to immerse yourself in the region's unique ecosystems and witness the diverse flora and fauna that call this area home. The Barrens Trail, in particular, provides a captivating journey through coastal heathlands, granite outcrops, and windswept forests. As you hike along the trail, keep an eye out for wildlife such as white-tailed deer, various bird species, and even seals playing in the distance.

The panoramic views of the Atlantic Ocean from the trails and viewpoints within the park are nothing short of breathtaking. From elevated vantage points, you can take in the vast expanse of the ocean, its azure waters stretching as far as the eye can see. The rugged cliffs and rocky islands dotted along the coastline add to the dramatic beauty of the landscape, creating a scene that is both awe-inspiring and humbling. Whether you're capturing stunning photographs or simply taking a moment to soak in the natural splendor, the views at Crystal Crescent Beach Provincial Park will leave a lasting impression.

For outdoor enthusiasts, Crystal Crescent Beach Provincial Park offers a variety of recreational activities. Fishing enthusiasts can try their luck casting their lines into the ocean, hoping to reel in a catch of mackerel or cod. The park is also a popular destination for kayaking and paddleboarding, allowing visitors to explore the calm waters and hidden coves at their own pace. With the pristine conditions and the picturesque backdrop, these water-based activities offer a unique perspective of the park's coastal beauty.

To make the most of your visit to Crystal Crescent Beach Provincial Park, consider packing a picnic and enjoying a meal amidst nature's splendor. There are several picnic areas with tables and grills where you can gather with friends and family, savoring delicious food while surrounded by the park's tranquil ambiance. As you indulge in your meal, take in the panoramic views and listen to the symphony of crashing waves, immersing yourself fully in the beauty of your surroundings.

When planning your visit to Crystal Crescent Beach Provincial Park, it's important to come prepared. Remember to bring sunscreen, as the sun's rays can be strong, and pack insect repellent, especially if you plan to explore the trails or have a picnic. Additionally, be mindful of the tides, as they can vary throughout the day, and it's essential to be aware of the water conditions before swimming.

Crystal Crescent Beach Provincial Park truly offers a serene escape from the city, allowing visitors to reconnect with nature and bask in the unspoiled beauty of the Atlantic coastline. Whether you choose to lounge on the soft sands, explore the scenic trails, or simply take in the breathtaking views, this hidden gem of Halifax is sure to leave a lasting impression. As you immerse yourself in the tranquil ambiance and embrace the natural wonders that surround you, Crystal Crescent Beach Provincial Park will undoubtedly become a cherished memory of your time in Nova Scotia.

Duncan's Cove Coastal Trail: Scenic Hiking and Ocean Vistas

For avid hikers and nature enthusiasts, the Duncan's Cove Coastal Trail presents an exhilarating adventure along the rugged coastline near Halifax. Stretching for approximately 7 kilometers (4.3 miles), this scenic trail winds its way through a mix of coastal forests, granite cliffs, and picturesque coves, offering a captivating journey for those seeking to immerse themselves in Halifax's natural beauty.

The trailhead for Duncan's Cove Coastal Trail is located just a short drive from downtown Halifax, making it easily accessible for both locals and visitors. As you begin your hike, you'll immediately be greeted by the invigorating scent of saltwater mingling with the earthy aroma of the surrounding forest. The trail is well-marked and maintained, ensuring a safe and enjoyable experience for hikers of all levels.

The journey along Duncan's Cove Coastal Trail is a feast for the senses. The rustling of leaves underfoot, the distant sound of crashing waves, and the gentle sea breeze all contribute to the immersive ambiance of the trail. The trail meanders through lush coastal forests, where towering trees provide shade and a habitat for a variety of bird species. Keep an eye out for woodpeckers, warblers, and even the occasional bald eagle soaring overhead.

As you continue along the trail, you'll reach the first glimpse of the mesmerizing coastline. The rugged cliffs, sculpted by the relentless pounding of the Atlantic Ocean, offer a dramatic backdrop to the trail. Granite boulders, weathered by centuries of exposure to the elements, line the path, providing both a challenge and a sense of awe for hikers. Take your time to navigate the rocky terrain, allowing yourself to be captivated by the raw power and beauty of the coastal landscape.

One of the highlights of the Duncan's Cove Coastal Trail is the breathtaking panoramic views of the Atlantic Ocean that unfold as you progress further along the path. With each step, the vista expands, revealing the endless expanse of sparkling blue waters stretching towards the horizon. The sight is truly awe-inspiring and serves as a reminder of the vastness and grandeur of the ocean.

Throughout the hike, you'll encounter fascinating rock formations that have been shaped by the relentless forces of wind and water. These geological wonders add a touch of intrigue to the trail, inviting hikers to explore their crevices and marvel at their unique shapes and textures. In certain areas, you may even come across tide pools teeming with marine life, offering a glimpse into the diverse ecosystem that thrives along the coast.

One of the most memorable experiences along the Duncan's Cove Coastal Trail is the opportunity to spot seals basking on the rocks. As you approach certain sections of the coastline, keep a keen eye out for these playful creatures, as they often use the rocky outcrops as a resting place. Witnessing seals in their natural habitat is a magical sight, and it serves as a reminder of the abundant wildlife that calls the Halifax coastline home.

The trail offers varying difficulty levels, allowing hikers to choose the section that suits their preferences and abilities. For those seeking a moderate hike, the initial stretch of the trail offers a good balance of natural beauty and manageable terrain. As you venture further, the trail becomes more challenging, with steep ascents and descents along the rugged cliffs. These sections reward hikers with even more breathtaking views, but they require caution and careful footing. It's important to wear appropriate footwear and take breaks as needed to ensure a safe and enjoyable experience.

Whether you're a seasoned hiker or a novice explorer, Duncan's Cove Coastal Trail provides a memorable adventure that showcases the untamed beauty of Halifax's coastline. It's a trail that allows you to connect with nature, appreciate the power of the ocean, and find solace in the serenity of the coastal forests. As you hike along the trail, take the time to pause, breathe in the salty sea air, and savor the moments of tranquility that this captivating outdoor experience offers.

Remember to come prepared for your hike along the Duncan's Cove Coastal Trail. Pack plenty of water, snacks, and sunscreen to stay hydrated and protected from the sun's rays. It's also advisable to bring a camera or smartphone to capture the stunning vistas and wildlife encounters along the way. Finally, respect the natural environment by staying on designated trails, carrying out any trash, and leaving no trace of your visit.

Duncan's Cove Coastal Trail is a testament to the natural wonders that can be found just a stone's throw away from Halifax's urban center. It offers a chance to escape the hustle and bustle of city life and embark on a journey that will leave you with lasting memories of Halifax's breathtaking coastal beauty. Lace up your hiking boots, embrace the spirit of adventure, and get ready to be enchanted by the wonders of Duncan's Cove Coastal Trail.

Lawrencetown Beach: Surfers' Paradise and Coastal Beauty

Just a short drive east of Halifax lies Lawrencetown Beach, a captivating destination that beckons surfers and beach lovers alike. Renowned for its impressive waves and consistent swells, this expansive sandy beach has gained popularity among surfers from around the region and beyond. However, Lawrencetown Beach offers much more than just a surfer's paradise. It serves as a scenic retreat for those seeking solace amidst nature, providing a perfect opportunity to stroll along the shore, breathe in the fresh ocean air, and marvel at the raw power of the mighty Atlantic Ocean.

Lawrencetown Beach stretches along the eastern coastline of Nova Scotia, spanning approximately 1.5 kilometers. As you approach the beach, you'll be greeted by the rhythmic crashing of waves against the shore, creating an atmosphere of serenity and excitement. The wide expanse of sandy beach invites visitors to bask in the sunshine, build sandcastles, or simply relax and enjoy the picturesque surroundings.

Surfers are drawn to Lawrencetown Beach for its exceptional wave conditions. The beach is known to produce impressive swells, making it a popular destination for experienced surfers seeking thrilling rides. The consistent wave action, particularly during the fall and winter months, attracts surfers of all skill levels who are eager to test their abilities on the challenging Atlantic waves. If you've ever wanted to learn to surf, Lawrencetown Beach also offers surf schools and rentals, providing an opportunity to embark on an exhilarating surfing adventure under the guidance of experienced instructors.

Even if you're not catching waves, Lawrencetown Beach offers a captivating experience for all visitors. As you wander along the shore, you'll be mesmerized by the sheer beauty of the surroundings. The vast expanse of ocean stretching to the horizon, the sound of seagulls soaring overhead, and the gentle breeze carrying the scent of saltwater all contribute to an atmosphere of tranquility and natural wonder.

Lawrencetown Beach is not only a haven for surfers and beachgoers but also a paradise for birdwatchers. The coastline is home to numerous species of shorebirds that thrive in the intertidal zones and feed on the rich marine life found in the area. As you explore the beach, you may spot majestic seagulls gliding gracefully through the air, sandpipers scurrying along the water's edge, and the occasional osprey soaring high above, scanning the waters for their next meal. Birdwatchers will find themselves captivated by the diversity of avian life that calls Lawrencetown Beach home.

Beyond the sandy shoreline, Lawrencetown Beach offers a backdrop of rugged cliffs and rolling hills, adding to the scenic allure of the area. Nature enthusiasts can embark on hikes along the adjacent trails that wind their way through coastal forests, providing breathtaking views of the beach and the vastness of the Atlantic Ocean. These trails offer an opportunity to connect with the natural beauty of the region, observe the local flora and fauna, and revel in the serenity of the coastal landscape.

Lawrencetown Beach is not only a place of natural beauty but also an important site for environmental conservation. The beach and surrounding area are protected, ensuring the preservation of its unique ecosystems. The dunes and marshlands that border the beach provide crucial habitats for a variety of plant and animal species, contributing to the overall ecological health of the region. Visitors are encouraged to respect and appreciate the natural environment by adhering to responsible beach practices, such as staying on designated trails, disposing of trash properly, and avoiding any disturbances to the fragile coastal ecosystem.

Whether you're a surfer seeking the thrill of riding Atlantic waves, a beach lover in search of a serene retreat, a birdwatcher captivated by coastal avian life, or a nature enthusiast drawn to the rugged beauty of the shoreline, Lawrencetown Beach offers an unforgettable experience. It is a place where the power of the ocean meets the tranquility of the sandy shores, creating a harmonious blend of natural wonders. A visit to Lawrencetown Beach is a chance to connect with the elements, embrace the beauty of the

Atlantic coastline, and immerse yourself in the captivating allure of Halifax's natural splendor.

In Halifax, outdoor adventures are abundant, allowing travelers to connect with nature and experience the region's breathtaking landscapes. Whether you're exploring the urban trails of Point Pleasant Park, marveling at the iconic Peggy's Cove lighthouse, venturing into the wilderness of McNabs Island, or embarking on a whale watching excursion, Halifax's natural beauty promises unforgettable outdoor experiences for all.

Where to Eat: Culinary Delights of Halifax

Halifax is a haven for food lovers, offering a diverse culinary scene that showcases the region's bountiful seafood, international flavors, craft breweries, and local produce. Here are some highlights of the city's culinary delights:

Seafood Extravaganza: Fresh Catches and Lobster Feasts

When it comes to seafood, Halifax truly stands out as a paradise for seafood lovers. Situated along the Atlantic Ocean, the city boasts a vibrant and thriving fishing industry, ensuring that the seafood you enjoy here is as fresh as it gets. From succulent lobster to mouthwatering scallops, Halifax offers a plethora of dining options that cater to every seafood enthusiast's palate.

For an unforgettable seafood experience, the waterfront area is the perfect place to start your culinary journey. Here, you'll find upscale restaurants that not only offer stunning views of the harbor but also a wide variety of seafood dishes prepared with creativity and flair. Immerse yourself in the maritime ambiance as you savor the catch of the day while overlooking the shimmering waters.

One iconic seafood dish that should not be missed during your visit to Halifax is the lobster roll. This delicacy features tender, juicy chunks of fresh lobster meat nestled in a buttery, toasted roll. Whether you prefer it served warm with melted butter or chilled with a tangy mayonnaise-based dressing, the lobster roll is a quintessential maritime delight that encapsulates the taste of the Atlantic.

If scallops are your weakness, Halifax has got you covered. The city takes pride in its abundance of plump, sweet scallops, which are expertly seared to perfection. Whether they are served as an appetizer, a main course, or paired with other seafood delights, Halifax's scallops are sure to leave a lasting impression on your taste buds.

To truly experience the breadth of Halifax's seafood offerings, indulge in a traditional Maritime seafood platter. These generous platters feature a delightful assortment of ocean treasures, showcasing the region's rich culinary heritage. From succulent lobster tails and juicy shrimp to tender crab legs and briny oysters, each bite is a celebration of the sea's bounty. Accompanied by tangy cocktail sauce, zesty lemon wedges, and perhaps a side of buttery garlic sauce, a seafood platter promises an explosion of flavors and textures.

Beyond the waterfront, Halifax is home to numerous seafood-focused establishments that cater to all tastes and budgets. From cozy family-run seafood shacks to trendy seafood bistros, there is a dining spot for everyone. Explore the charming neighborhoods of Halifax and stumble upon hidden gems where you can enjoy fresh fish and chips, hearty seafood chowder, or even innovative seafood creations that fuse local ingredients with international flavors.

When dining in Halifax, it's not just the quality of the seafood that shines but also the culinary expertise and dedication of the local chefs. With their passion for showcasing the region's finest ingredients, these talented culinary artists transform simple seafood into unforgettable culinary experiences. The flavors are enhanced by innovative techniques, creative combinations of ingredients, and a deep respect for the traditions of maritime cooking.

To complement your seafood feast, Halifax also offers an impressive selection of local wines and craft beers. Pair your meal with a crisp white wine produced by one of the nearby vineyards, or opt for a locally brewed ale that complements the rich flavors of the seafood. The knowledgeable staff at the restaurants and breweries are often more than happy to recommend the perfect beverage pairing to elevate your dining experience.

For those interested in learning more about Halifax's seafood heritage, consider embarking on a culinary tour or a seafood-focused cooking class. These experiences provide an opportunity to not only sample various seafood dishes but also gain insights into the fishing industry, the importance of sustainable practices, and the art of preparing seafood like a local.

In conclusion, Halifax's reputation as a seafood paradise is well-deserved. With its proximity to the Atlantic Ocean, the city offers a wide array of fresh catches and seafood delicacies that cater to every palate. Whether you're savoring a succulent lobster roll, indulging in perfectly seared scallops, or delighting in a bountiful seafood platter, the culinary delights of Halifax's seafood scene are sure to leave you with a deep appreciation for the ocean's bounty and a taste of maritime magic.

North End Eateries: Hip Cafes and International Flavors

Nestled in the heart of Halifax, the North End stands out as a vibrant neighborhood bursting with culinary delights. This eclectic area is renowned for its trendy eateries, cozy brunch spots, and innovative restaurants that fuse global flavors with locally sourced ingredients. Whether you're a foodie seeking authentic Italian pasta, tantalizing Middle Eastern dishes, or daring fusion creations that push the boundaries of taste, the North End promises an unforgettable dining experience that caters to every palate.

As you venture into the North End, you'll be greeted by charming streets lined with an array of restaurants, cafes, and bistros, each with its own unique character and culinary offering. The neighborhood exudes a welcoming atmosphere, drawing locals and visitors alike to explore its diverse gastronomic scene.

For those craving traditional Italian cuisine, the North End boasts several establishments that serve up mouthwatering pasta, wood-fired pizzas, and delectable antipasti. Step into a rustic trattoria and savor the aromas of garlic, basil, and simmering tomato sauce that fill the air. Indulge in homemade gnocchi, perfectly al dente spaghetti, or creamy risotto prepared with seasonal ingredients. Each bite transports you to the sun-soaked landscapes of Italy, showcasing the culinary prowess and dedication of Halifax's talented Italian chefs.

If you're in the mood for flavors from the Middle East, the North End delivers with its array of Lebanese, Moroccan, and Turkish eateries. Immerse yourself in the vibrant colors and aromatic spices that characterize these cuisines. Feast on tender lamb skewers, fragrant couscous, and sumptuous falafel wraps. Let the richness of tahini and the tang of za'atar tantalize your taste buds as you savor the authentic flavors of the Levant. The North End's Middle Eastern establishments offer a delightful escape to the bustling streets of Beirut or the bustling souks of Marrakech.

For the adventurous food lover, the North End presents a playground of culinary innovation. Here, you'll find chefs who fearlessly combine diverse culinary traditions, resulting in fusion creations that both surprise and delight. Prepare to embark on a culinary journey where boundaries are blurred, and flavors are reinvented. Taste the marriage of Asian and Latin American cuisines, where tangy Korean kimchi meets savory Mexican tacos. Experience the harmonious fusion of Indian spices with Canadian ingredients, creating a symphony of flavors that reflect the multicultural fabric of Halifax.

Beyond the diverse range of restaurants, the North End is also home to charming cafes that offer a cozy retreat and a chance to savor a perfect cup of coffee or tea. These hip establishments showcase the local coffee culture, emphasizing specialty brews, ethically sourced beans, and skilled baristas who turn coffee-making into an art form. Take a moment to relax in a welcoming cafe, sip a freshly brewed cappuccino, and soak in the neighborhood's creative energy.

As you navigate the North End's culinary landscape, be sure to explore the hidden gems that lie off the beaten path. Wander through the neighborhood's side streets and discover unassuming eateries that may surprise you with their exceptional flavors and intimate settings. These hidden culinary treasures often showcase the true essence of

Halifax's gastronomic creativity, allowing you to experience the city's culinary scene from a fresh and authentic perspective.

The North End's culinary offerings are a testament to Halifax's vibrant and diverse food culture. The neighborhood's talented chefs, restaurateurs, and baristas work tirelessly to create memorable dining experiences that celebrate both local ingredients and global influences. Whether you're a connoisseur of traditional flavors or an adventurous epicurean, the North End promises a culinary journey that will leave you inspired, satisfied, and craving more.

So, venture into Halifax's North End, and let your taste buds guide you through a world of gastronomic wonders. Embrace the creativity, flavors, and warmth that define this culinary haven. From cozy brunch spots to inventive fusion restaurants, the North End beckons you to embark on a culinary adventure that will forever be etched in your memory. Bon appétit!

Halifax Brewery Scene: Craft Brews and Tastings

Beer enthusiasts will find themselves in hoppy heaven when visiting Halifax, as the city boasts a thriving craft brewery scene that is sure to delight even the most discerning palate. With numerous microbreweries and brewpubs dotting the cityscape, Halifax has become a destination for those seeking unique and flavorful beers that showcase the passion and creativity of local brewers.

One of the best ways to fully immerse yourself in Halifax's beer culture is by taking a brewery tour. These tours offer an opportunity to go behind the scenes and learn about the brewing process, from selecting the finest ingredients to the careful fermentation and bottling stages. Knowledgeable guides will take you on a journey through the art and science of brewing, sharing fascinating insights and stories along the way. You'll gain a deeper appreciation for the craftsmanship and dedication that goes into every pint.

During brewery tours, sampling a variety of brews is a highlight for beer enthusiasts. Halifax's craft breweries pride themselves on their diverse offerings, catering to a range of tastes and preferences. Whether you're a fan of hoppy IPAs that explode with citrusy flavors and piney aromas, crave the robust and velvety experience of a rich stout, or seek the refreshing crispness of a well-crafted ale, Halifax's brewery scene has something to satisfy every beer lover.

The breweries in Halifax showcase an array of styles and flavors, showcasing the creativity and innovation of local brewers. From traditional recipes that pay homage to classic beer styles to bold experiments that push the boundaries of taste, each sip tells a story and captures the essence of Halifax's brewing community.

One notable aspect of Halifax's craft brewery scene is the passion and dedication of the brewers themselves. These artisans pour their heart and soul into their craft, constantly experimenting with new ingredients, refining their techniques, and striving for perfection. When you visit a brewery, you not only get to taste their creations but also have the opportunity to engage with the brewers themselves. They are often more than happy to share their knowledge, answer questions, and provide insights into their brewing philosophy. It's a chance to connect with the people behind the beer, fostering a sense of community and appreciation for the craft.

As you embark on a journey through Halifax's brewery scene, you'll discover a variety of establishments, each with its own unique ambiance and character. Some breweries feature spacious taprooms where you can enjoy your beer while chatting with friends or playing board games, while others offer cozy brewpubs that combine the comfort of a pub with the excitement of on-site brewing. The atmosphere is often lively and welcoming, creating an ideal setting to enjoy great beer and engage in conversations with fellow beer enthusiasts.

While touring the breweries, keep an eye out for special events and collaborations. Halifax's beer community frequently hosts beer festivals, tap takeovers, and collaborations between breweries. These events are an excellent opportunity to experience a wide range of beers in one place, sample limited-edition brews, and witness the camaraderie and collaborative spirit that thrives within the industry. It's a chance to celebrate the vibrant beer culture of Halifax and interact with fellow enthusiasts and industry professionals.

In addition to the brewery tours and taproom experiences, Halifax is also home to beer-focused bars and establishments that offer an extensive selection of local and international brews. These beer bars pride themselves on curating diverse and ever-changing tap lists, showcasing the best beers from Halifax's breweries and beyond. It's a haven for those seeking new and exciting flavors, as well as a place to discover hidden gems and rare finds.

Beyond the liquid gold that fills the glasses, Halifax's craft brewery scene is also deeply intertwined with the local community and the region's rich history. Many breweries collaborate with local farmers and suppliers, sourcing ingredients from nearby farms and embracing the farm-to-glass philosophy. This commitment to supporting local producers not only ensures the freshness and quality of the beer but also contributes to the sustainability and growth of the local economy.

In conclusion, Halifax's craft brewery scene offers beer enthusiasts an unforgettable journey into the world of unique and flavorful brews. Whether you embark on a brewery tour, enjoy the vibrant taproom experiences, or explore the curated selections of beer bars, you'll be captivated by the passion, creativity, and camaraderie that defines Halifax's beer community. So raise your glass, savor the distinct flavors, and toast to the vibrant beer culture that awaits in this coastal gem of Nova Scotia. Cheers!

Farmers' Markets: Local Produce and Artisanal Goods

For a taste of Halifax's local flavors, immerse yourself in the vibrant and lively atmosphere of the city's farmers' markets. These bustling hubs of culinary delights offer a diverse array of fresh, locally grown produce, artisanal goods, and homemade treats that showcase the rich agricultural heritage of the region. Among the must-visit markets in Halifax, the Halifax Seaport Farmers' Market stands out as a popular destination that captures the essence of the city's vibrant food culture.

Situated on the waterfront, the Halifax Seaport Farmers' Market is a bustling marketplace that showcases the best of what the region has to offer. As you approach the market, you'll be greeted by a lively ambiance and the enticing aromas of freshly baked bread, aromatic spices, and brewing coffee. The market's vibrant atmosphere is fueled by the energy and passion of the local vendors who take pride in their products and are eager to share their knowledge and stories with visitors.

One of the highlights of the Halifax Seaport Farmers' Market is the wide selection of vendors offering an impressive variety of products. From the moment you step inside, you'll be captivated by the colorful displays of fruits and vegetables, all locally grown and bursting with flavor. From plump and juicy berries to crisp greens and vibrant root vegetables, the market is a haven for those seeking the freshest and most nutritious produce.

As you explore further, you'll discover stalls offering an enticing range of artisanal goods. Local cheese makers proudly display their handcrafted cheeses, each with its own distinct flavor and character. Delicate wedges of creamy brie, sharp cheddars, and tangy goat cheeses are just a sample of the offerings that await. Pair your cheese selection with freshly baked bread, made with care and expertise by talented local bakers who infuse their creations with love and creativity. The aroma of warm, crusty loaves and the sight of golden pastries will tempt your taste buds and make it impossible to resist indulging in a savory treat.

The Halifax Seaport Farmers' Market also celebrates the sweet side of life. Artisanal chocolate makers showcase their velvety creations, ranging from classic flavors to innovative combinations that push the boundaries of taste. Indulge in a piece of rich, dark chocolate or savor the delicate sweetness of a handcrafted truffle. For those with a sweet tooth, the market is a treasure trove of homemade desserts and pastries. Delight in freshly baked pies bursting with seasonal fruits, buttery croissants that melt in your mouth, or decadent cupcakes adorned with intricate designs.

Engaging with the friendly vendors is an integral part of the farmers' market experience. They are not only passionate about their products but also knowledgeable about the origins and production methods behind them. Strike up a conversation, ask questions, and learn about the journey of the food from farm to market. The vendors' stories and insights will deepen your appreciation for the local flavors and the hard work that goes into bringing them to your plate.

Beyond the products themselves, the Halifax Seaport Farmers' Market offers a unique opportunity to connect with the community. The market serves as a gathering place for locals and visitors alike, fostering a sense of camaraderie and shared appreciation for quality food. It's a place where conversations flow freely, recommendations are exchanged, and a sense of belonging is cultivated. Join the bustling crowd, take a seat at a communal table, and enjoy the vibrant atmosphere as you savor the flavors of Halifax.

Visiting the Halifax Seaport Farmers' Market is not only a delightful culinary experience but also an opportunity to support local farmers and producers. By purchasing from these dedicated individuals, you directly contribute to the sustainability of the local food system and the livelihoods of those who work tirelessly to bring fresh, high-quality products to the market. It's a chance to embrace the farm-to-table ethos and make a positive impact on the community.

In conclusion, a visit to one of Halifax's vibrant farmers' markets, such as the Halifax Seaport Farmers' Market, is an essential part of experiencing the local flavors and embracing the culinary culture of the city. Explore the stalls, engage with the friendly vendors, and immerse yourself in the bustling atmosphere as you discover a diverse range of fresh produce, artisanal goods, and homemade treats. Indulge in the flavors that reflect the region's agricultural heritage, and support the local community by choosing to savor the fruits of their labor. The Halifax Seaport Farmers' Market is a place where culinary exploration meets community connection, creating lasting memories and a deeper appreciation for the vibrant food culture of Halifax.

Indulging in Halifax's culinary delights is a journey of flavors and experiences. Whether you're savoring a seafood extravaganza, exploring the North End's eclectic eateries, sampling craft brews, or browsing the farmers' markets for local treasures, you'll discover the true essence of Halifax's diverse and delicious food scene. Bon appétit!

Practical Information: Tips and Resources for a Memorable Trip

Best Time to Visit Halifax

Determining the best time to visit Halifax depends on various factors, including your preferences, the type of experiences you seek, and the seasonal highlights that interest you. Halifax experiences distinct seasons throughout the year, each offering unique attractions and activities. Let's explore each season in more detail to help you make an informed decision about when to plan your visit.

Summer (June to August): Festivals, Outdoor Delights, and Vibrant Atmosphere

Summer is the peak tourist season in Halifax, and for good reason. The city comes alive with a vibrant atmosphere, bustling streets, and a plethora of festivals and outdoor events. The pleasant weather, with average temperatures ranging from 17°C to 25°C (63°F to 77°F), makes it an ideal time to explore the city's many attractions.

One of the highlights of summer in Halifax is the Halifax International Busker Festival, a renowned street performance festival that showcases talented artists from around the world. The waterfront comes alive with mesmerizing performances, from acrobatics to music and comedy, creating an atmosphere of excitement and entertainment.

The summer months are perfect for exploring the picturesque waterfront boardwalk, where you can stroll along the harbor, visit the shops and galleries, and enjoy waterfront dining with stunning views. You can also embark on boat tours and cruises to explore the surrounding islands and coastal beauty.

Outdoor enthusiasts will delight in the numerous activities available during summer. You can go kayaking or paddleboarding in the harbor, take a scenic hike in Point Pleasant Park, or enjoy a beach day at one of the nearby sandy shores. Halifax is also a popular destination for golfing, with several excellent courses to choose from.

Seafood lovers will find their cravings satisfied during the summer months. Halifax boasts an abundance of fresh seafood, and you can indulge in delicious lobster, scallops, and other maritime delicacies at the city's many seafood restaurants and lobster shacks.

Spring (April to May) and Fall (September to October): Mild Temperatures and Scenic Beauty

Spring and fall are considered shoulder seasons in Halifax, offering milder temperatures, fewer crowds, and an opportunity to enjoy the city's natural beauty in a more serene setting.

In spring, the temperatures start to warm up, ranging from 5°C to 15°C (41°F to 59°F). The city begins to awaken from winter, and you can witness the blossoming of cherry trees and other spring flowers in public gardens and parks. It's a lovely time to explore Halifax's historic sites and museums without the summer crowds.

Fall in Halifax is a true visual delight as the leaves transform into vibrant hues of red, orange, and gold. The temperatures gradually cool down, ranging from 10°C to 20°C (50°F to 68°F), creating a comfortable atmosphere for outdoor activities and exploration. Peggy's Cove, a picturesque fishing village near Halifax, is particularly enchanting during this time, with the fall colors adding an extra layer of beauty to its rugged coastal landscapes.

Fall is also harvest season in Nova Scotia, and you can visit local farmers' markets to sample fresh produce, artisanal goods, and locally crafted beverages. The Annapolis Valley, known for its apple orchards and wineries, is a scenic day trip option from Halifax, where you can partake in apple picking and wine tastings.

Winter (November to March): Festive Celebrations and Winter Sports

Winter in Halifax brings a magical atmosphere, festive celebrations, and opportunities for winter sports enthusiasts. However, it's important to note that winter in Halifax can be cold, with temperatures ranging from -3°C to 3°C (27°F to 37°F), and occasional snowfall.

Despite the cold weather, Halifax embraces the winter season with open arms. The city transforms into a winter wonderland, adorned with holiday lights, festive decorations, and cheerful vibes. The Halifax Lights Festival brightens up the city's downtown area with stunning light installations, creating a magical ambiance for evening strolls.

Winter sports enthusiasts will find plenty to enjoy in Halifax. You can go ice skating at the Emera Oval, a large outdoor rink located in the heart of the city. Skiing and snowboarding enthusiasts can head to nearby Martock or Wentworth, where they can hit the slopes and enjoy winter activities.

The holiday season in Halifax is filled with festive markets, concerts, and events. The Halifax Christmas Market offers a charming experience with local vendors selling crafts, gifts, and seasonal treats. You can also attend concerts and performances by local artists, choirs, and theater groups that celebrate the holiday spirit.

In conclusion, determining the best time to visit Halifax depends on your preferences and the experiences you seek. Summer is the peak tourist season with vibrant festivals and outdoor activities, while spring and fall offer milder temperatures and stunning scenery. Winter brings festive celebrations and opportunities for winter sports enthusiasts. Consider your interests, weather preferences, and the type of atmosphere you desire, and plan your visit accordingly to make the most of your time in Halifax.

Accommodations: Where to Stay in Halifax

Halifax, the vibrant coastal city in Nova Scotia, offers a wide range of accommodation options that cater to various budgets and preferences. Whether you're seeking luxurious hotels, charming boutique accommodations, or budget-friendly hostels, Halifax has something for everyone.

Downtown Halifax: Central Location and Vibrant Atmosphere

Downtown Halifax is a popular choice for visitors due to its central location and bustling atmosphere. This area is home to many of the city's major attractions, shopping districts, restaurants, and nightlife. Staying in downtown allows for easy access to popular landmarks like the historic Citadel Hill, the scenic Halifax Waterfront Boardwalk, and the vibrant entertainment district on Argyle Street. You'll find a diverse selection of accommodations, ranging from high-end hotels with stunning harbor views to stylish boutique hotels with unique designs. Many of these establishments provide excellent amenities, including on-site restaurants, fitness centers, and spa facilities. Downtown Halifax is a hub of activity, making it an ideal choice for travelers who want to be at the heart of the city's vibrant energy.

North End: Laid-Back Setting with Local Charm

If you prefer a more laid-back and residential atmosphere, consider staying in Halifax's North End. This area is known for its charming neighborhoods, local eateries, and an artsy vibe. You'll find beautifully restored heritage homes, colorful row houses, and independent shops and galleries that showcase the local artistic talent. The North End is also home to some fantastic dining options, with a focus on farm-to-table cuisine, craft breweries, and cozy cafes. Agricola Street, in particular, is a food lover's haven, offering an array of culinary delights. Staying in the North End provides a glimpse into the local community and a chance to immerse yourself in the neighborhood's unique character.

Clayton Park, Bedford, and Dartmouth: Suburban Comforts

For those seeking a suburban feel and convenient access to shopping centers and recreational activities, areas like Clayton Park, Bedford, and Dartmouth offer excellent options. These neighborhoods are situated a short distance from downtown Halifax, providing a quieter and more relaxed atmosphere. Accommodations in these areas often include comfortable hotels and well-appointed vacation rentals. If you're traveling with family or prefer a more spacious setting, these suburban areas may be an ideal choice. Clayton Park offers a variety of amenities, including shopping malls and parks, while Bedford boasts picturesque waterfront views and a charming downtown core. Dartmouth, located across the harbor, features a mix of historical sites, scenic trails, and vibrant local shops. These areas provide a balance between suburban comfort and easy access to Halifax's main attractions.

Research and Booking in Advance

Regardless of which area you choose to stay in, it is advisable to research and book your accommodation in advance, especially during peak seasons. Halifax attracts a significant number of visitors, particularly during the summer months when festivals and events are in full swing. Booking in advance ensures you have a wider selection of options and increases the likelihood of securing your preferred accommodations. It's also worth considering flexibility in your travel dates, as rates may vary depending on the time of year and any special events taking place in the city.

In addition to the location and ambiance of your chosen accommodation, consider factors such as amenities, proximity to public transportation, and parking availability if you plan to rent a car. Many hotels offer complimentary Wi-Fi, fitness centers, and on-site dining options, while others may provide perks like complimentary breakfast or shuttle services.

When it comes to finding and booking accommodation in Halifax, there are several popular apps and websites that can help simplify the process. Here are some widely used platforms for searching and booking accommodations in Halifax:

Booking.com: Booking.com is a well-known platform that offers a wide range of accommodation options, including hotels, apartments, and guesthouses. The platform provides user reviews, detailed property descriptions, and flexible booking options.

Airbnb: Airbnb is a popular platform that allows individuals to rent out their homes, apartments, or rooms to travelers. It offers a range of unique and local accommodation options, including entire homes, private rooms, and shared spaces.

Hotels.com: Hotels.com specializes in hotel bookings and provides a vast selection of hotels in Halifax. The platform offers user reviews, hotel descriptions, and competitive prices. It also has a rewards program that allows you to earn free nights with your bookings.

Expedia: Expedia is a comprehensive travel platform that allows you to search and book flights, hotels, and rental cars. It offers a wide range of accommodation options in Halifax, along with user reviews and competitive pricing.

TripAdvisor: TripAdvisor is a popular travel website that not only provides reviews and recommendations for attractions and restaurants but also offers a hotel booking feature. It allows you to search for accommodations in Halifax based on your preferences and provides user-generated reviews and ratings.

Trivago: Trivago is a hotel search and comparison platform that allows you to compare prices from multiple booking sites. It provides an overview of available accommodations in Halifax and helps you find the best deals based on your preferences.

Kayak: Kayak is a comprehensive travel search engine that allows you to search for flights, hotels, and rental cars. It aggregates information from various booking sites, including accommodations in Halifax, allowing you to compare prices and find the best options.

These apps and websites are widely used and trusted by travelers to find and book accommodations in Halifax. It's recommended to explore multiple platforms to compare prices, read reviews, and find the best fit for your preferences and budget.

Ultimately, the choice of where to stay in Halifax depends on your preferences and the kind of experience you seek. Whether you opt for the vibrant atmosphere of downtown, the laid-back charm of the North End, or the suburban comforts of Clayton Park, Bedford, or Dartmouth, Halifax's diverse accommodations ensure there's a perfect place to rest and rejuvenate after your exciting adventures in this coastal gem.

Transportation: Getting In and Around the City

By Air:

Halifax Stanfield International Airport (YHZ) is the primary airport serving the city of Halifax and the wider region of Nova Scotia. Located approximately 35 minutes from downtown Halifax, it offers excellent connectivity with domestic and international destinations. The airport is well-equipped to handle a large volume of passengers and provides a range of amenities to ensure a comfortable travel experience.

With multiple airlines operating at Halifax Stanfield International Airport, travelers have a variety of options when it comes to choosing their flights. Major Canadian carriers such as Air Canada, WestJet, and Porter Airlines offer regular domestic flights to and from Halifax, connecting the city to various destinations across the country. Additionally, several international airlines provide direct flights to Halifax from major cities in the United States, Europe, and other parts of the world.

Upon arrival at Halifax Stanfield International Airport, passengers can easily access downtown Halifax using various transportation options. Car rental services are available at the airport for those who prefer to have their own vehicle during their stay. Additionally, taxis and ride-sharing services are readily available, providing convenient and efficient transportation to downtown Halifax and other areas of interest.

For travelers who prefer public transportation, the airport offers bus services operated by Halifax Transit. The Airport Express bus service connects the airport to downtown Halifax, with multiple stops along the way. This is a cost-effective option for those looking to reach their accommodations or explore the city using public transit.

By Car:

Halifax is easily accessible by car, thanks to its connection to the Trans-Canada Highway (Highway 102). The Trans-Canada Highway serves as a major artery, linking Halifax to other parts of Nova Scotia, as well as neighboring provinces such as New Brunswick and Prince Edward Island.

Travelers coming from the north or south can reach Halifax by driving along Highway 102. From the north, Highway 102 connects Halifax to Truro, where it intersects with Highway 104, providing access to northern Nova Scotia and New Brunswick. From the south, Highway 102 extends from the

Greater Halifax Area to the border with the United States in Amherst.

Driving to Halifax offers the flexibility to explore the scenic landscapes and charming towns along the way. The highways are well-maintained, and there are several rest areas and gas stations available for drivers to take breaks and refuel. It's important to familiarize yourself with the driving regulations in Nova Scotia, including speed limits, seat belt laws, and other road rules, to ensure a safe and enjoyable journey.

Once in Halifax, there are various parking options available for visitors. Most hotels offer on-site parking or have partnerships with nearby parking facilities. Additionally, there are public parking lots and street parking available throughout the city. However, it's essential to pay attention to parking signs and regulations to avoid any fines or towing.

Public Transportation:

Halifax boasts an efficient and comprehensive public transportation system, operated by Halifax Transit. Buses serve as the primary mode of public transportation within the city, covering most areas and providing a convenient way to get around.

Halifax Transit operates numerous bus routes that connect different neighborhoods, commercial areas, and major attractions. The buses are equipped with modern amenities such as comfortable seating, wheelchair accessibility, and real-time GPS tracking, making it easy for travelers to navigate the city. The transit system operates on a schedule, and buses arrive at designated stops at regular intervals. Schedules and route maps are available online and at various transit hubs and information centers.

One of the unique features of Halifax's public transportation system is the ferry service. The ferry connects downtown Halifax to Dartmouth, a neighboring city across the harbor. This short but scenic journey offers stunning views of the waterfront and is a popular mode of transportation for both residents and visitors. The ferry service operates throughout the day, with frequent departures, allowing travelers to easily explore both sides of the harbor.

To make traveling by public transit more convenient, Halifax Transit offers reloadable transit cards. These cards, known as "HFX Transit Farecards," can be purchased and loaded with funds, allowing passengers to enjoy discounted fares and easy transfers between buses and ferries. The cards can be reloaded at various locations, including convenience stores, transit terminals, and online.

Taxis and Ride-Sharing:

For those who prefer a more direct and convenient mode of transportation, taxis and ride-sharing services are readily available in Halifax. Taxis can be found at designated taxi stands throughout the city or can be hailed on the street. Additionally, many hotels and popular tourist areas have taxi services readily available.

In recent years, ride-sharing services such as Uber and Lyft have become increasingly popular in Halifax. These app-based services provide a convenient and often more affordable alternative to traditional taxis. Travelers can simply download the app, request a ride, and have a driver pick them up at their desired location.

Taxis and ride-sharing services are ideal for shorter trips within the city or for those who prefer the convenience of door-to-door transportation. They are particularly useful for late-night outings or when traveling with heavy luggage. It's important to note that fares may vary depending on factors such as distance, time of day, and demand.

Overall, Halifax offers a range of transportation options to cater to the diverse needs of travelers. Whether you prefer the convenience of flying, the flexibility of driving, the affordability of public transit, or the directness of taxis and ride-sharing, getting in and around Halifax is a seamless experience. Choose the mode of transportation that suits your preferences and enjoy exploring the charming coastal gem of Nova Scotia.

Essential Phrases and Local Customs

English is the primary language spoken in Halifax. However, you may encounter some local slang and regional accents. Here are a few essential phrases to enhance your experience:

"Hello" - "Hi" or "Hello"

"Thank you" - "Thank you" or "Thanks"

"Please" - "Please"

"Excuse me" - "Excuse me" or "Pardon me"

"Where is...?" - "Where is...?"

"Goodbye" - "Goodbye" or "Bye"

Halifax is known for its friendly and welcoming atmosphere. It's customary to greet others with a smile and engage in polite conversation. Tipping is also a common practice in restaurants, bars, and for taxi drivers. The standard tip is around 15-20% of the total bill.

Respecting the local customs and cultural heritage is important. Be mindful of historical sites and exhibits, follow posted rules and regulations, and show consideration for the environment and local communities.

Conclusion

As we conclude our journey through the "Halifax Travel Guide: Discover the Charms of Nova Scotia's Coastal Gem," it becomes abundantly clear that Halifax is a city that captures the hearts of all who visit. From its rich history to its vibrant culture, Halifax offers a tapestry of experiences that leave a lasting impression on travelers.

Throughout this guide, we have unveiled the captivating allure of Halifax, showcasing its iconic landmarks such as Citadel Hill and the Maritime Museum of the Atlantic. We have strolled through the city's Victorian oasis, the Halifax Public Gardens, and explored the beautifully preserved Historic Properties. Each step we took was imbued with the weight of history, enveloping us in the stories of Halifax's past.

Yet, Halifax is not just a city frozen in time. It pulsates with a dynamic cultural scene, boasting the Art Gallery of Nova Scotia, Neptune Theatre, and the annual Halifax Jazz Festival. These institutions celebrate creativity and provide a platform for local and international artists to thrive, ensuring that visitors are immersed in a vibrant and ever-evolving cultural landscape.

One cannot speak of Halifax without mentioning its spectacular waterfront. The Halifax Waterfront Boardwalk offers breathtaking views of the harbor, while the Canadian Museum of Immigration at Pier 21 tells the powerful stories of those who arrived on Canadian shores. The harbor itself comes alive during the Tall Ships events, where majestic vessels grace the waters, reminding us of Halifax's seafaring heritage.

For those seeking outdoor adventures, Halifax does not disappoint. Point Pleasant Park beckons with its scenic trails, while Peggy's Cove enchants with its picturesque fishing village and iconic lighthouse. McNabs Island invites intrepid explorers to venture into untouched wilderness, and whale watching tours offer unforgettable encounters with marine life. Halifax's natural beauty is a constant companion, inviting us to embrace the great outdoors.

And let us not forget the culinary delights of Halifax. From succulent seafood feasts to international flavors found in the North End eateries, the city's food scene tantalizes the taste buds. The thriving brewery scene and vibrant farmers' markets offer further opportunities to savor the local fare, ensuring that every meal becomes a memorable experience.

With practical tips and resources at your disposal, this guide empowers you to make the most of your visit to Halifax. From the best time to go to choosing accommodations and navigating transportation, you have the tools to create a seamless and unforgettable trip.

In conclusion, Halifax is a city that captivates with its history, culture, natural beauty, and culinary delights. It welcomes visitors with open arms, inviting them to immerse themselves in its rich heritage and experience the warmth and hospitality of its people. Whether you are a history buff, an outdoor enthusiast, a cultural explorer, or a food lover, Halifax offers something truly special. So pack your bags, embark on an adventure, and let Halifax leave an indelible mark on your heart and soul.

Made in the USA
Las Vegas, NV
29 April 2024

89296755R00066